BEST COOKBOOK EVER

MAX + ELI SUSSMAN

PHOTOGRAPHY **ERIN KUNKEL**
ILLUSTRATION **MATTHEW ALLEN**

OLIVE PRESS

CHOOSE YOUR OWN FOOD ADVENTURE

HANGOVER CURES 14

When you wake up and feel like death, don't call a doctor. You don't need a second opinion. You mixed some things together and you drank until it was light outside. So just follow our prescription: cook these recipes and you'll have a full belly and be feeling better in no time.

JUST ADD BACON 30

Even though we're not vegetarians, we definitely sort of, kind of accept people who are. It's like your decision, man. It's not exactly "cool" anymore, but hey, who are we to judge you? And if you do fall off the farmers' market wagon, you can follow our "meatification" suggestions at the end of each recipe.

DADDY NEEDS A SNACK 44

Hors d'oeuvres, snackies, canapés, snack 'ems, appateezees—call them what you will, but at their core, they are little bites of heaven. Angelic flavor wings deliver these tiny umami-packed nibbles to your mouth. So if you're throwing a classy affair, going over to someone's house for a dinner party, or just nostalgic for a bar mitzvah, turn to this chapter.

MY DRINKS LIKE TO PARTY ALL THE TIME 46

TASTY CHOICES BEFORE TASTELESS DECISIONS 64

What you do on your own time when the sun goes down is your own business. We're not Maury Povich trying to put you on blast. But hey, why not make something healthful and light, yet still filling and flavorful, before you go do something you will inevitably regret? (And when you wake up with an extreme need for a hangover cure, jump back to chapter one.)

JUST BECAUSE YOU DON'T HAVE FRIENDS DOESN'T MEAN YOU CAN'T MAKE DINNER 78

We wrote a whole chapter of recipes for when it's just you. Because you are beautiful and you deserve it. You'll also have great leftovers for lunch the next day.

CAPTAIN DINNER PARTY 94

Superheroes are all the rage right now. The 25th most-popular Marvel character is getting a franchise tent-pole blockbuster. In the spirit of ridiculous characters, we invented Captain Dinner Party. His motto? Cook like EVERYONE is watching. When you got it, flaunt it. So channel CDP and create some epic feasts for any occasion.

HOW TO THROW THE BEST PARTY EVER 110

NO REGRETS 136

These desserts are awesome. They are unlike any you will find in any other cookbook, anywhere in the entire world, throughout all of history, including the future. And the past. Conclude your food adventure here. Or start it here?!? *Gaboommm woosshhh.* That's the sound of your mind being blown. By dessert.

FILL A SWIMMING POOL FULL OF BREAD AND DIVE INTO IT 150

FOREWORD

Food is one of the world's great unsolved mysteries. What is it? An animal? Nope. You can't keep it as a pet. A vegetable? No again. Vegetables are stuck in the dirt, and food is on a plate. A mineral? Hmmm, I don't think so. Minerals are gems. Food is much less sparkly, and you can't propose to someone with a piece of food.

Historically, no one has ever known what food is or how to deal with it. "Can't live with it, can't live without it!" said Mahatma Gandhi about food, just before he went on a hunger strike. Isaac Newton was sitting under a tree when an apple fell on his head. He picked it up, said "I have no idea how to cook this into a pie," and cried himself to sleep.

I am completely dumbfounded when it comes to food. I don't know how to do anything in the kitchen. I am a 25-year-old woman and I can't even pay my taxes! (Note: if you're a government official, I actually can pay my taxes; sometimes I may even pay too much.) This is where the Sussmans come in. They're going to teach you and me what we've never been able to learn in the past. These nice Jewish boys (one is nicer than the other; I will reveal which one in a short quiz below) have put together everything we need to know to feed ourselves and our friends.

I need a book like this. I've tried to learn how to cook before, and it has not worked out. My family tried to teach me. My grandmother is an amazing cook. She can make a dessert out of nothing more than a box of red wine that she drinks and a store-bought cake! But nothing ever sunk in until I read this masterpiece. I've learned so much, like did you know that you're supposed to eat bacon? I thought it was a garnish, like parsley or plastic wrap. And did you know that books cost money? I was pretty sure they were like "take a penny, leave a penny" bins. You could take what you wanted from bookstores, and when you wrote a book, you'd just leave yours there. (Note: if you're a cop, I have never "stolen" a book; usually I overpay for them.)

You will love these boys! Yes, boys can cook, too. They have planned easy-to-make meals for every situation. Hangovers? Check. Brunches? Check. Entertaining? You'll never be caught with your pants down at a dinner party again. (I used to host dinner parties with no pants on to distract from the terrible food.) After this cookbook, you'll be able to create a perfect meal for all your cool friends and to pull your pants up casually at your leisure!

This book will change your life. You will start it as a starving, scared child and finish it as a confident adult with hundreds of friends and a subpoena from the IRS for not paying your taxes for the past six years. Best of luck, my friends! And don't forget to save room for dessert!

Oh, and the nicer one is Max. Or is it Eli? I can't remember. I'm very hungry now.

MEGAN AMRAM
comedy writer and American taxpayer

When we started writing this book, we had to ask ourselves, why would anybody want to cook anymore?

ELI Many of our friends go out to eat all the time (we're perhaps the most guilty of this), but we see cooking at home as a lost art making a tremendous comeback.

MAX And if you're reading this, it means that you still believe there's something incomparable about a home-cooked meal. We totally agree. Maybe you don't feel like spending the money, maybe it's the satisfaction of doing it yourself, maybe it's the desire to feel creative, or maybe you're like us and you actually just love to cook.

ELI Or maybe you just don't want to put on any clothes and leave your cozy apartment.

MAX We've based this cookbook around a bunch of true—and also totally-made-up, ridiculous—situations that you might find yourself in. 'Cause we've been there before. We came up with the chapters first and then filled in the recipes from there, so that each recipe fits in with a specific entertaining or personal situation. Real solutions. To real problems.

ELI It's time to stop reading now. Turn on the oven or fire up the grill or start heating the oil in that sauté pan.

MAX Fly, my child.

ELI Fly like a bird.

MAX Soar as high as the clouds. But beware of the sun.

ELI Shoot for the moon, because the worst you can do is land among the stars.

TOOLS WE LOVE AND THAT YOU SHOULD ACQUIRE OVER

1 **COTTON DISH TOWELS** 2 **CAST-IRON DUTCH OVEN** 3 **MANDOLINE** 4 **MICROPLANE GRATER** 5 **SILICONE SPATULA**
6 **MEASURING SPOONS** 7 **GLASS MEASURING CUP** 8 **LARGE SOUPSPOON FOR TASTING** 9 **FRYING PAN**

TIME TO MAKE YOUR KITCHEN THE BEST KITCHEN EVER

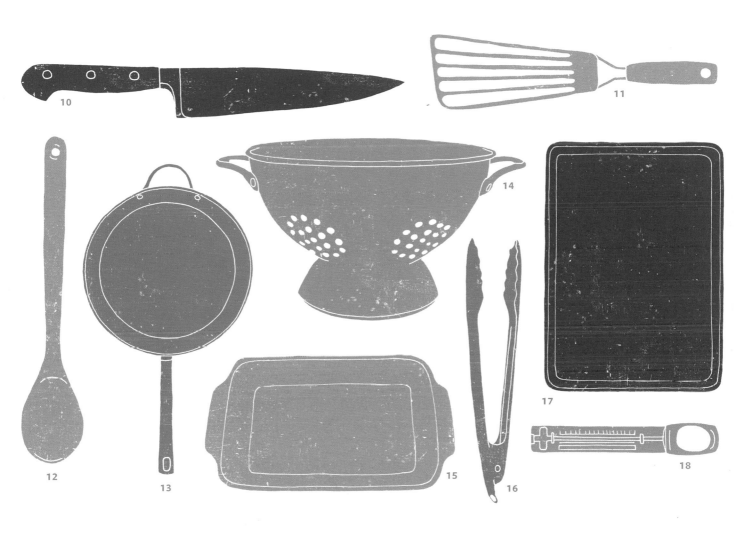

10 CHEF'S KNIFE **11** FISH SPATULA **12** WOODEN SPOON **13** SAUTÉ PAN **14** COLANDER **15** GLASS BAKING DISH
16 TONGS **17** HALF SHEET TRAY **18** CANDY THERMOMETER

HANGOVER CURES

Hangover Cures

We embrace our inner evil genius when it comes to being hungover. Remember that one Sunday way back in the day when you combined five different types of cereal in one bowl and you watched five hours of cartoons in your underwear because it's exactly what you wanted to do? These recipes are just like that but better. Free yourself from the constraints of a "socially acceptable breakfast option." Save your healthy granola for Monday morning. Welcome to weekend hangover nirvana. There's just no holding back in this chapter … Reach out for it. Grab it and invite friends over to partake in the spoils of these riches. Get as drunk as you want, and when you're ready for your friends to leave, just yawn and walk the 10 feet to your bed for your first nap of the day. They'll get the picture.

1 lb (500 g) Yukon gold potatoes, peeled and cut into ½-inch (12-mm) dice

Kosher salt

Extra-virgin olive oil, as needed

½ lb (250 g) Mexican Chorizo (page 153)

8 corn tortillas

2 Tbsp unsalted butter, at room temperature

8 large eggs

2 radishes, trimmed and thinly sliced

½ cup (¾ oz/20 g) chopped fresh cilantro leaves and stems

4 oz (125 g) cotija or Parmesan cheese, shredded (about 1 cup)

CHORIZO BREAKFAST TACOS

SERVES 4

This is a great standard and involves considerably less work than you think. It's so easy to wake up and fry eggs and put them on a tortilla. This recipe just adds more components to make it mind-blowingly delicious. I actually make this often in my life, and I am a well-adjusted, very happy, successful 30-year-old. Don't you want to be just like me? You can. Make this. — **Max**

Put the potatoes in a saucepan and add cold water to cover. Stir in 1 teaspoon salt and bring to a boil over high heat. Immediately drain in a colander set in the sink and rinse under cold running water. Transfer to paper towels and let drain, changing towels if necessary, until the potatoes are very dry and completely cool.

Heat a large, heavy-bottomed frying pan over medium-high heat. If your chorizo is very lean, drizzle a little olive oil into the pan to prevent it from sticking. Add the chorizo, spread evenly around the pan, and cook without stirring until nicely caramelized on the bottom, 3–5 minutes. Stir to get the uncooked parts in contact with the pan and continue cooking until all the meat is cooked through, about 5 minutes more. Using a slotted spoon, transfer to a large bowl. Set aside.

If the pan looks dry, add more oil and heat over medium-high heat. Spread the potatoes evenly around the pan. Cook, stirring and turning gently with a spatula, until golden brown on all sides, about 10 minutes. Add to the bowl with the chorizo and mix gently. Taste and adjust the seasoning.

Pour off any excess fat in the pan into a small heatproof bowl and reserve. Place the pan over medium heat. One at a time, add the tortillas and fry on each side until they soften and blister slightly, about 30 seconds per side. If the pan dries out, add a tiny bit of the reserved fat (or olive oil, if there wasn't any fat to reserve). Keep the tortillas warm by stacking them and wrapping them in a kitchen towel as they come out of the pan.

In a small nonstick frying pan, heat 1 teaspoon olive oil over medium heat. When the oil is hot, add a scant teaspoon of the butter and swirl the pan to mix the fats. Crack an egg into the pan and cook until the white is just set, about 3 minutes. Slide the egg carefully onto a platter. Repeat to cook the remaining eggs in the remaining butter, adding more oil as needed.

To assemble the tacos, place 2 warm tortillas on each plate and spoon a few tablespoons of the chorizo and potato mixture in the middle of each tortilla. Top each with a fried egg and radish slices. Finish with a big pinch of the cilantro and a sprinkle of the cheese. Serve right away. Repeat until your hangover is gone or you can't eat anymore and take a nap.

FRIED CHICKEN SANDWICH WITH WATERMELON HOT SAUCE

SERVES 4

Here's one of the most popular brunch items I've ever run at Mile End Brooklyn. It's a no-brainer masterpiece that features the perfect summer-day pairing. The only way to improve on perfection is to transform it into a sandwich. The watermelon hot sauce gives a sweet kick that elevates this sandwich to something that haunts your brunch-craving dreams. At 1:00 a.m. on Friday night, I want you to be dreaming of the next morning when you get to wake up and eat this beauty. — Eli

Watermelon Hot Sauce
1 seedless watermelon, about 4 lbs (2 kg)
1 cup (8 oz/250 g) sugar
4 Tbsp Sriracha

Fried Chicken
4 boneless chicken thighs, preferably skin-on
2 cups (16 fl oz/500 ml) buttermilk
Vegetable oil for deep-frying

3 cups (3 oz/90 g) corn flakes
¾ cup (3 oz/90 g) panko bread crumbs
6 Tbsp (2¼ oz/70 g) all-purpose flour
1 Tbsp sweet paprika
1½ tsp kosher salt
1½ tsp red pepper flakes
Pickled Rinds (page 152)
4 hamburger buns, split and toasted

To make the hot sauce, remove the flesh from the watermelon rind (remember, reserve the rind for pickling!). Roughly chop the flesh, place in a food processor, and process until it forms a liquid. You should have about 4 cups (32 fl oz/1 l).

In a heavy saucepan, combine the watermelon liquid and sugar and bring to a boil over medium-high heat, stirring to dissolve the sugar. Reduce to a simmer and continue to cook, stirring often to prevent scorching, until reduced by half, about 45 minutes. Add the Sriracha, stir well, and remove from the heat. Let cool completely, then cover and refrigerate. (The sauce will keep for up to 2 weeks.)

To make the fried chicken, in a bowl, immerse the chicken thighs in the buttermilk and let soak for at least 15 minutes or up to 1 day in the refrigerator.

Pour oil to a depth of 5 inches (13 cm) into a deep pot or a deep fryer and heat to 335°F (170°C).

While the oil is heating, in the food processor, process the corn flakes until reduced to the consistency of the panko. Add the panko, flour, paprika, salt, and pepper flakes and pulse to combine. Transfer the mixture to a large bowl.

When the oil is ready, one at a time, remove the chicken pieces from the buttermilk, letting them drip a bit, then toss them in the crumb mixture until well coated. Carefully lower the chicken pieces into the hot oil and fry until deep golden brown on the outside and cooked through, 5–8 minutes; the timing depends on the thickness. Test for doneness with an instant-read thermometer; it should register 165°F (74°C). Using a wire skimmer or tongs, transfer the chicken to paper towels to drain briefly.

To assemble each sandwich, arrange a layer of rinds on the bottom of a bun and top with a piece of chicken. Drizzle 1 tablespoon of the hot sauce over the chicken and close with the bun top. Serve right away. Pass the remaining hot sauce at the table for anyone who would like more.

SMOKED SALMON SOFT SCRAMBLED EGGS

SERVES 4–6

This is the easiest recipe in the entire cookbook. Not only is it perfect for a group but it's also simple to scale down for one person. Tell everyone you're having them over for brunch. Buy the orange juice and the bagels and make these eggs. Then have your friends bring the lox, Champagne, and gin (you know, the pricey stuff).

12 large eggs

4 Tbsp (2 oz/60 g) unsalted butter

4 oz (125 g) pastrami lox, broken into bite-size pieces

¼ cup (2 oz/60 g) crème fraîche

¼ tsp kosher salt

¼ cup (⅓ oz/10 g) very thinly sliced fresh chives

Toasted rye bread for serving

In a large bowl, whisk the eggs until well blended. In a saucepan over low heat, melt the butter. Pour in the eggs and, using a silicone spatula, begin stirring. Stir constantly until you start to see some curds form, about 10 minutes. Keep the heat low and keep stirring until the mixture starts to resemble pudding, another 5–7 minutes or so. The goal is to cook the eggs as slowly as you can stand it. Your patience will be rewarded.

After about 15 minutes total time, the eggs should be thick enough so that when you scrape the spatula through them and against the pan bottom, you can see the pan for a few seconds. At that point, stir in the pastrami lox, crème fraîche, salt, and half of the chives. Heat just until the crème fraîche and lox are warmed through. (If the lox cooks too long, it will become dry.)

Spoon the eggs onto plates and garnish with the remaining chives. Serve right away with the toast.

Citrus Maple Syrup

1 cup (8 fl oz/250 ml) fresh orange juice

Grated zest of 1 orange

Grated zest of 1 lemon

¾ cup (8 fl oz/250 g) pure maple syrup

⅓ cup (1½ oz/45 g) whole-wheat flour

1 cup (5 oz/155 g) all-purpose flour

⅓ cup (2 oz/60 g) buckwheat flour

⅓ cup (1½ oz/45 g) medium-grind cornmeal

3 Tbsp sugar

2 tsp baking powder

½ tsp baking soda

1 tsp kosher salt

1 large egg

1¾ cups (14 fl oz/430 ml) whole milk

4 Tbsp (2 oz/60 g) unsalted butter, melted and cooled, plus extra at room temperature for cooking

WHOLE-WHEAT SILVER DOLLAR PANCAKES WITH CITRUS MAPLE SYRUP

SERVES 4

These remind me of the delicious pancakes our dad made when we were younger. Pancakes are the type of thing you always remember as being better than they are, so here is our attempt to create one that's even better than what you remember. The Sussman brothers: eliciting positive childhood memories through food since 2011, cheaper than a shrink and with fewer tissues (but perhaps more napkins). — Max

To make the syrup, in a small saucepan, simmer the orange juice over medium-low heat until it thickens, caramelizes, the bubbles get smaller, and it is reduced to 2–3 tablespoons, about 15 minutes. As the orange juice cooks down, reduce the heat as needed to keep it from burning. To test for doneness, pour a small spoonful of the reduced juice onto a chilled plate in the refrigerator. It should be viscous, with a consistency similar to honey or maple syrup.

When the syrup is done, let cool slightly, then stir in the zests and the maple syrup. Cover to keep warm and set aside while you make the pancakes. (The syrup will keep, tightly covered in the refrigerator, for up to 2 weeks.)

In a bowl, whisk together the flours, cornmeal, sugar, baking powder, baking soda, and salt. Set aside.

In a large bowl, beat together the egg, milk, and melted butter. Add the dry ingredients to the wet ingredients and stir until just barely mixed; the mixture should remain lumpy.

Heat a frying pan over medium heat. Add a few teaspoons of the room-temperature butter. Swirl the pan until the butter is melted and the bottom is evenly coated. Drop the batter by the heaping tablespoon into the pan, spacing the spoonfuls about ½ inch (12 mm) apart. Cook until bubbles appear in the middle of each pancake, 2–3 minutes. Flip the pancakes and cook until brown on the second side, 1–2 minutes longer. Lift each pancake with the corner of the spatula to see if it is ready. Transfer the pancakes to a heatproof platter and keep them warm in a low oven while you cook the remaining pancakes.

Serve the pancakes warm, with the syrup on the side.

½ small carrot, peeled

½ Persian or ¼ English cucumber, peeled and seeded

½ jalapeño or serrano pepper (the serrano will give more heat)

2 small radishes, thinly sliced

1 Tbsp rice vinegar

½ tsp brown sugar

Grated zest of 1 lemon

Kosher salt

2 slices firm tofu, each about ½ inch (12 mm) thick, 2 inches (5 cm) wide, and as long as the tofu block

2 Tbsp vegetable oil

One 10-inch (25-cm) soft demi baguette (not a crusty French baguette) or Italian roll

1 Tbsp extra-virgin olive oil

1 Tbsp unsalted butter

2 large eggs, beaten

1 Tbsp minced fresh cilantro stems

2 green onions, white and tender green parts only, trimmed and thinly sliced

Kewpie mayo, for spreading

¼ cup (¼ oz/7 g) packed fresh cilantro leaves

Sriracha to taste

FRIED TOFU BÁNH MÌ OMELET

SERVES 1

There is a *bánh mì* shop a block away from our house that is damn good and mighty cheap. We've spent many a ragged hungover morning zombie walking there with Murphy, Max's dog, to pick up food. One time we wondered why there wasn't a breakfast *bánh mì*. Crispy bread, hot eggs, spicy sauce—sounds perfect, right? Our shop didn't have it, so we made it ourselves. For the best *bánh mì*, you want to use a fresh Italian roll, fluffy inside, white bread. Don't make this on whole wheat and e-mail us saying you didn't love it. We will publicly shame you.

Preheat the oven to 350°F (180°C).

Cut the carrot, cucumber, and hot pepper into julienne about ⅛ inch (3 mm) wide and 3 inches (7.5 cm) long (a mandoline is ideal for this). Put the julienned vegetables in a bowl and add the radishes, vinegar, brown sugar, lemon zest, and ½ teaspoon salt. Toss to mix well. Let sit at room temperature for at least 20 minutes.

Dry the tofu well with paper towels and season lightly on both sides with salt. In a frying pan, heat the vegetable oil over medium heat. When the oil is hot, add the tofu slices and fry, turning once, until golden brown and crispy, about 3 minutes per side. Transfer to paper towels to drain.

Toast the baguette in the oven for 5 minutes.

While the baguette is toasting, heat the olive oil in a small nonstick frying pan over medium heat. When the oil is hot, add the butter and swirl the pan to blend the fats. Add the eggs and a pinch of salt, reduce the heat to low, and let cook undisturbed. When you see curds starting to form, using a silicone spatula, stir the eggs quickly. Repeat until about two-thirds of the eggs are cooked. At this point, spread the eggs out evenly and sprinkle the cilantro stems and green onions over the top. Let cool until the eggs are just barely set. Don't worry about making the omelet perfect, since it's going to be folded into the sandwich.

Split the baguette horizontally but stop just short of cutting all the way through, to leave a joint on one side. Spread mayo on the cut side of the baguette bottom. Using the silicone spatula, carefully roll the omelet onto itself and then out of the pan onto the baguette. Cover with the cilantro leaves, pickled vegetables, tofu, Sriracha, and more mayo, if desired. Serve right away.

BAKED POTATO CHILI HASH

SERVES 4

This is an absurd recipe—hash browns with chili with a half pound of bacon and a pound of ground beef. It's what everyone really wants for breakfast when they are hungover but are too ashamed to order the separate components at a restaurant and assemble it on the table. Meat. Cheese. Potato. Eat it . . . then take a nap . . . until tomorrow.

3 russet potatoes, peeled and cut into small dice (about 4 cups/1¼ lb/625 g)

2 Tbsp extra-virgin olive oil

Kosher salt

Super-Quick Chili

1 tsp vegetable oil

1 lb (500 g) ground beef

2 tsp chipotle chile powder

2 tsp chili powder

1 tsp ground cumin, or more to taste

½ tsp cayenne pepper

¼ tsp ground coriander

1 can (15 oz/470 g) whole tomatoes, with juice, roughly crushed with your hands

4 oz (125 g) sharp Cheddar cheese, shredded (about 1 cup)

½ lb (250 g) bacon, cooked until crisp and chopped

1 cup (8 oz/250 g) sour cream

1 bunch green onions, white and tender green parts only, trimmed and thinly sliced

Preheat the oven to 425°F (220°C).

Put the potatoes in a saucepan and add cold water to cover. Bring to a boil over high heat. Immediately drain in a colander set in the sink and rinse under cold running water. Drain again thoroughly, then transfer to a large bowl and toss with the olive oil and a pinch of salt. Spread the potatoes in an evenly spaced single layer on a sheet tray. Roast, stirring once or twice, until crispy and golden brown, 30–40 minutes. Remove from the oven; leave the oven on.

While the potatoes are cooking, make the chili: In a heavy-bottomed frying pan, heat the vegetable oil over medium-high heat until smoking. Add the beef and cook, stirring occasionally and using your spoon to break up the meat, until browned, about 5 minutes. Add the chipotle and chili powders, cumin, cayenne, and coriander and stir to mix well. Cook for about 2 minutes to toast the spices a little. Add the tomatoes with their juices. Bring to a simmer, then reduce the heat to medium-low and cook until slightly thickened, about 30 minutes. Taste and adjust the seasoning and spice level.

Transfer the potatoes to a 9-inch (23-cm) square baking dish. Spoon the chili into the dish and spread evenly. Sprinkle the cheese evenly over the top. Bake until the cheese is melted, about 10 minutes.

Let cool slightly, then garnish with the bacon, sour cream, and green onions and serve right away.

3 Tbsp unsalted butter,
at room temperature

4 slices brioche, each
about 1 inch (2.5 cm) thick

4 oz (125 g) Parmesan cheese,
grated (about 1 cup)

2 slices extra-sharp Cheddar cheese,
at room temperature

4 oz (125 g) Camembert cheese,
at room temperature, broken into
small pieces

4 Tbsp (3 oz/75 g) Spicy Tomato Jam
(page 153)

GRILLED CHEESE WITH
SPICY
TOMATO JAM

Preheat the oven to 350°F (180°C).

Spread a thin layer of butter on one side of each bread slice. Sprinkle the buttered sides with the Parmesan, dividing it evenly, and shake off the excess.

Turn 2 of the bread slices butter-and-Parmesan side down. Top each slice with a slice of Cheddar, then half of the Camembert, and finally 2 tablespoons of the jam, adding the jam in small dollops. Close the sandwiches with the remaining 2 bread slices, buttered side up.

Heat an ovenproof nonstick or cast-iron frying pan over medium heat. When the pan is hot, place the sandwiches in the pan (do not crowd them; if your pan is small, cook them one at a time). After 3 minutes, check to see if the first side is a deep golden brown; it may need another minute. When nicely browned, flip the sandwiches and cook until golden brown on the second side, about 3 minutes longer.

Transfer the pan to the oven and bake until the cheese has melted, another 3 minutes or so. Let cool slightly, then cut in half and serve warm.

MAKES 2 LARGE SANDWICHES

There is grilled cheese on the outside of this grilled cheese. You've now reached the point in this book where you've caught on to the fact that we are absolutely not fucking around. This is inspired by the astounding sandwich that chef April Bloomfield does at The Breslin. She's a genius.

JUST ADD BACON

Just Add Bacon Okay, we know there are bona fide, real-life vegetarians out there. And that is totally cool. This chapter's for you! So all of you actual vegetarians, skip this intro, turn the page immediately, and cook. Enjoy! … Okay, they're gone now, so we can speak freely. Listen up all you people who have said any of the following: "I'm mostly vegetarian." "I'm a vegetarian but I eat chicken." "I'm a vegetarian but I eat fish sometimes." We know your secret. You eat animals and enjoy it. Often. It's okay. We won't tell. But when you reach those pearly gates and Jesus looks you in the eye, he's gonna know you're not actually a vegetarian. This chapter's also for you. In every recipe we give a suggestion for easy meatification. So you can have your cake (made of beef) and eat it too.

PEARL COUSCOUS SALAD WITH POMEGRANATE SYRUP

SERVES 4

We love pearl couscous because the texture is more like pasta than like a grain. Equally perfect for summertime outside or wintertime indoors and also delicious served hot or cold, the true trick to elevating this dish is the pomegranate syrup. We obviously suggest making your own (you are in fact reading a cookbook with recipes). But in the case that you are in a rush or lazy (we are assuming that you're most likely American and therefore you are both), a lot of specialty grocers will carry pomegranate molasses in the Middle Eastern section.

2 cups (16 fl oz/500 ml) pomegranate juice

1 tsp light brown sugar

Kosher salt

About ½ cup (4 fl oz/120 ml) extra-virgin olive oil

1 cup (6 oz/185 g) pearl couscous

½ head cauliflower, cored and broken into small florets

¾ lb (375 g) cherry tomatoes

½ cup (2 oz/60 g) julienned red onion

Roasted Garlic Dressing (page 152)

3 oz (90 g) baby arugula

In a saucepan over medium heat, combine the pomegranate juice and brown sugar and bring to a gentle simmer, stirring to dissolve the sugar. Reduce the heat to low and cook until the juice is reduced to 2–3 tablespoons syrup, about 30 minutes. Set the pomegranate syrup aside.

In a saucepan, bring 1¼ cups (10 fl oz/310 ml) water to a boil over high heat. Stir in ½ teaspoon salt and about 2 tablespoons of the olive oil. Pour in the couscous, stir once, and reduce the heat to low. Cover tightly and let simmer for 10 minutes. Uncover and stir with a spoon, then cover again until ready to use.

While the couscous is simmering, in a large sauté pan, heat about ¼ cup (2 fl oz/60 ml) of the olive oil over high heat. Add the cauliflower and a pinch of salt and sauté until the cauliflower is dark around the edges but not completely tender, 3–5 minutes. Using a slotted spoon, transfer to paper towels to drain. Return the pan to high heat and add the tomatoes to the residual olive oil. Add another 1 tablespoon oil if the pan seems dry. Cook until the skins are blistered, 2–3 minutes. Remove from the heat.

In a large bowl, combine the couscous, cauliflower, tomatoes, onion, and dressing and toss to mix well. Taste and adjust the seasoning. Add the arugula and toss gently to combine. Place on a serving platter and finish with a drizzle of the pomegranate syrup. Serve right away.

MEATIFICATION Leaving on a meat plane from vegetarianism and don't know when you'll be back again? Add pulled cumin-rubbed roasted lamb shoulder.

1 Tbsp peeled and grated fresh ginger

2 Tbsp soy sauce

1 Tbsp toasted sesame oil

1 Tbsp rice vinegar

1 Tbsp Sriracha

1 Tbsp white sesame seeds

1½ lb (750 g) seedless watermelon, rind removed, cut into 1-inch (2.5-cm) dice (about 2 cups/ 10 oz/315 g)

1 Tbsp olive oil

1 bunch green onions, tough tops and any discolored leaves removed, ends trimmed

1 tsp black sesame seeds

GINGER - SESAME WATERMELON SALAD

SERVES 2

In a large bowl, combine the ginger, soy sauce, sesame oil, vinegar, Sriracha, and white sesame seeds and stir to mix well. Add the watermelon and toss gently to coat with the dressing. Set aside.

In a frying pan, heat the olive oil over medium-high heat. Fill a small stockpot with water. When the oil is hot, lay the green onions in the pan, arranging them in a single layer so they aren't touching. Place the stockpot in the frying pan on top of the onions, to weight them and press them into contact with the pan bottom. Cook until the onions are charred on the edges and bottom, about 1 minute. Remove from the heat and set aside.

Using a slotted spoon, transfer the watermelon from the bowl to individual plates. Ladle about 1 tablespoon of the dressing left in the bowl over the top. Sprinkle over the black sesame seeds and charred green onions and serve right away.

MEATIFICATION Beefing up with protein to remain competitive in your underground fight club? Serve with crispy sliced roasted duck breast.

Normally you only see watermelon cut up on the fruit platter next to unripe cantaloupe and the ravaged strawberry section. Here, we take the Paul Walker of fruit and elevate it to Vin Diesel status by adding a salty sesame marinade. By making watermelon the focal point, you can convince anyone that a big hunk of meat is not always necessary for a blockbuster salad. They won't even have the ability to disagree because they'll be furiously stuffing their faces with this dish. Fast. They'll be eating it fast. And furious.

CRISPY RICE WITH BROCCOLI
AND TERIYAKI SAUCE

SERVES 2–4

Isn't this just a stir-fry you ask? Oh sorry … was Sir Paul McCartney just a singer? We were discussing how we are obsessed with the crispy rice at the bottom of a sizzling stone bowl of *bibimbap*. So here's a whole dish centered around those crunchy golden nuggets of perfect rice crisps. A note on mirin: it's a sweetened rice wine and it's worth seeking out to get the flavor of this recipe right. It's pretty tough to replicate the flavor using other ingredients, and since it makes this recipe special, expand your culinary horizons and pick up a bottle.

1 cup (7 oz/220 g) jasmine rice

6 Tbsp (3 fl oz/90 ml) olive oil

4 oz (125 g) shiitake mushrooms, brushed clean, stems removed, and torn into 1-inch (2.5-cm) pieces

1 cup (2 oz/60 g) broccoli florets

1 Tbsp soy sauce

Teriyaki Sauce (page 152)

1 bunch green onions, white and tender green parts only, thinly sliced

To make the crispy rice, in a wide saucepan with a tight-fitting lid, combine the rice and 2 cups (16 fl oz/500 ml) water and bring to a boil over high heat. Reduce the heat to maintain a simmer, cover, and set your timer for 12 minutes. Do not remove the lid. After 12 minutes, remove from the heat. Let the rice stand, still covered, without disturbing for 10 minutes.

Preheat the oven to 200°F (95°C). Use a paper towel or your hands to spread 2 tablespoons of the olive oil on a sheet tray. Spread the rice evenly on the pan and pat it down with a silicone spatula. Bake until dry, 30–45 minutes.

In a large nonstick frying pan, heat 2 tablespoons of the olive oil. When the oil is hot, add the mushrooms and broccoli and sauté until the mushrooms are softened slightly and nicely caramelized, and the broccoli is crisp-tender, 3–5 minutes. Add the soy sauce, stir to combine, and transfer the vegetables to a bowl and set aside.

Wipe out the pan and heat the remaining 2 tablespoons olive oil over medium heat. Carefully add the rice to the pan, leaving it in big clumps (about 4 inches/10 cm in diameter) and fry until it puffs up slightly and becomes crispy, 3–4 minutes. Turn the rice patties over once, to crisp on the underside, then transfer to a plate. Repeat with the remaining rice.

To serve, place a few large chunks of crispy rice on a serving plate and top with the broccoli and shiitake mushrooms. Drizzle with some of the teriyaki sauce, sprinkle with the green onions, and serve right away.

MEATIFICATION Stowing away on a cross–Atlantic journey for a better nonvegetarian life? Add crispy braised and seared pork belly.

1 kabocha squash

2 Tbsp extra-virgin olive oil

Kosher salt

Celery Vinaigrette

3 Tbsp extra-virgin olive oil

2 Tbsp cider vinegar

¼ cup (¼ oz/7 g) fresh flat-leaf parsley leaves

½ tsp celery seeds

Kosher salt

1 small head radicchio, cored, separated into leaves, and torn into 2–3 inch (5–7.5-cm) pieces

1 small bunch lacinato kale, as young as possible, stems and tough central spines removed, and leaves torn into 2–3 inch (5–7.5-cm) pieces

1 cup (4 oz/125 g) frozen peeled and cooked chestnuts, thawed

3 ribs celery, cut on the diagonal into slices about ¼ inch (6 mm) thick

Inner leaves of 1 head celery

ROASTED WINTER SQUASH WITH CHESTNUTS KALE, RADICCHIO, AND CELERY VINAIGRETTE

SERVES 4–6

Preheat the oven to 350°F (180°C). Line a sheet tray with parchment paper.

Cut the squash in half. Scrape out the seeds and stringy membranes with a spoon. Brush the cut sides with the olive oil and sprinkle evenly with 1 teaspoon salt. Place on the prepared pan, cut side down, and sprinkle with ¼ cup (2 fl oz/60 ml) water. Bake until tender, about 45 minutes. Remove from the oven and let cool.

To make the vinaigrette, in a blender, combine the olive oil, vinegar, parsley, celery seeds, and ½ teaspoon salt and process to a smooth purée. Refrigerate until ready to serve.

Remove the skin from the squash and discard. Cut the flesh into roughly 2-inch (5-cm) chunks and put in a large bowl. Add the radicchio, kale, chestnuts, celery ribs, and celery leaves. Pour in the vinaigrette and toss gently to mix. Taste and adjust the seasoning. Serve right away.

MEATIFICATION Sneaking away from your vegetarian home and hitchhiking to a meatopian paradise? Add spiced roasted pork loin.

This is an expertly crafted combination of delectable vegetables. Even though you may be thinking holy shit there are a lot of vegetable ingredients in this, we promise that together they will sing quite unlike anything you've ever witnessed, unless you just came from a performance by the Boys Choir of Harlem. If you can't find chestnuts, leave them out. It's still going to taste harmonious.

PUFF PASTRY
WITH POTATOES
SMOKED PAPRIKA
SPINACH AND CHÈVRE

MAKES 9 PIECES

If we were rappers, we'd drop a single called "Starch on Starch," because honestly, we don't live within the confines of normal society. Rules are for chumps. And do we look like chumps? Rhetorical question. The point of this recipe is that it's a vegetarian dish that will fill you up. The true danger here is that you'll make it for a dinner party and eat the whole thing outta the oven, rendering yourself a useless pile of shame on the kitchen floor, rubbing your belly and whispering "sorry, not sorry" over and over.

1½ lb (750 g) small red-skinned potatoes, scrubbed but not peeled, cut into ¾-inch (2-cm) dice

¼ cup (2 fl oz/60 ml) extra-virgin olive oil, plus 1 Tbsp

Kosher salt

5 oz (155 g) baby spinach leaves

½ cup (4 fl oz/125 ml) heavy cream

¼ cup (2 oz/60 g) crème fraîche

2 tsp smoked paprika

1 package (14 oz/440 g) puff pastry, thawed

4 oz (125 g) fresh goat cheese

1 large egg

Preheat the oven to 425°F (220°C). Line a sheet tray with parchment paper. Have ready a second sheet tray.

Put the potatoes in a saucepan and add cold water to cover. Bring to a boil over high heat. Immediately drain in a colander set in the sink and rinse under cold running water. Drain again thoroughly, then transfer to a large bowl and toss with the ¼ cup (2 fl oz/60 ml) olive oil and a pinch of salt. Spread the potatoes in an evenly spaced single layer on the unlined sheet tray. Roast, stirring once or twice, until crispy and golden brown, 30–40 minutes. Remove from the oven.

In a sauté pan, warm the 1 tablespoon olive oil over medium-high heat. Add the spinach and sauté until wilted, 1–2 minutes. Put the spinach and roasted potatoes in a large bowl and let cool slightly, then add the cream, crème fraîche, and paprika and fold in until well blended.

On a lightly floured work surface, roll out the puff pastry into a 12-inch (30-cm) square. Cut the square into 9 equal pieces. Place about ¼ cup (2 oz/60 g) of the potato mixture on each square and spread evenly, leaving a border of about ½ inch (12 mm) along each edge. Dot the filling with the goat cheese, dividing it evenly. Working along the perimeter of each pastry, pinch the sides up and slightly over the filling, so the outside edge of the filling is covered but the filling is still visible in the center of the pastry. (It's okay if it looks a little weird.) Arrange on the parchment-lined sheet tray and place in the freezer for 10 minutes.

In a small bowl, beat the egg with 2 tablespoons water until well blended. Remove the pan from the freezer and brush each pastry with the egg wash. Bake until the pastries are dry to the touch and deep golden brown, 30–40 minutes. Let cool slightly, then serve.

MEATIFICATION Taking a vegetarian *Rumspringa*? Add bacon. Add a lot of bacon. Also, learn how to use a computer.

1 cup (7 oz/220 g) black lentils, picked over for stones or grit

3 Tbsp extra-virgin olive oil

1 yellow onion, minced

1 large clove garlic, minced

1-inch (2.5-cm) piece fresh ginger, peeled and minced

2 Tbsp curry powder, preferably homemade (page 153)

Kosher salt

½ lb (250 g) carrots, peeled and cut into 1-inch (2.5-cm) pieces

½ cup (¾ oz/20 g) chopped fresh mint

½ cup (¾ oz/20 g) chopped fresh cilantro

4 Tbsp plain yogurt (optional)

CURRIED LENTILS WITH ROASTED CARROTS AND MINT

SERVES 4–6

Preheat the oven to 450°F (230°C). Rinse and drain the lentils.

In a saucepan, heat 2 tablespoons of the olive oil over medium heat. Add the onion and cook, stirring often, until slightly softened, about 5 minutes. Add the garlic and ginger, reduce the heat to low, and continue cooking until all of the aromatics are soft, about 10 minutes. Add the curry powder and ½ teaspoon salt and cook, stirring, until the curry smells warm and slightly toasted, 2–3 minutes longer.

Add the lentils and 2 cups (16 fl oz/500 ml) water. Raise the heat to high and bring to a boil. Reduce the heat to low again and simmer until the lentils are just tender, 20–25 minutes.

Meanwhile, put the carrots on a sheet tray and toss with the remaining 1 tablespoon olive oil and a generous pinch of salt. Roast until golden brown around the edges and slightly softened, about 25 minutes.

When the lentils are cooked, remove from the heat and toss in the mint and cilantro. Taste and adjust the seasoning; you may want more curry powder for kick.

To serve, place a scoop of the lentils in the middle of each bowl. Arrange the roasted carrots over the lentils, dividing them evenly. Dollop the yogurt on top, if using, and serve right away.

MEATIFICATION Taking a trip on the meat express to carnivore town? Add thin slices of rare roasted lamb and finish with some spicy olive oil and black pepper.

Curry has hit the mainstream. These days you can find a lentil salad either in the cold case or prepackaged in the "organics" aisle at any fancy grocery store. We can assure you that both are terrible. Why? Because they are not fresh and there will always be a lack of seasoning in order to appeal to the greatest number of sheeple (that's *sheep+people* for the uninitiated). We aren't afraid of intense flavor and you shouldn't be either. The ease of cooking will delight you, the flavors will wow you, and the visual of it will surprise you. It's perfect. Yeah, we said it.

RIGATONI PAPRIKASH

SERVES 4

This is a take on a dish that we made at Zingerman's Deli in Ann Arbor. The exceptional chicken paprikash we made there was gluttonous and unforgettable. For this version, we use rigatoni in place of protein to maintain the original's hearty and filling nature. And since way back when our family came over from Hungary, we've got a soft spot in our heart for anything that's got paprika. — **Max**

Kosher salt

½ bunch kale, trimmed, torn into bite-size pieces

2 Tbsp olive oil

2 red bell peppers, seeded and cut into julienne

1 small yellow onion, cut into julienne

1 clove garlic, minced

2 Tbsp tomato paste

2 Tbsp unsalted butter

2 Tbsp all-purpose flour

1 cup (8 fl oz/250 ml) half-and-half

¾ cup (6 fl oz/180 ml) chicken broth

12 oz (375 g) aged Cheddar cheese, cut into ½-inch (12-mm) cubes

1 Tbsp Frank's RedHot cayenne pepper sauce

1 Tbsp smoked paprika

1 tsp sweet Hungarian paprika

¾ tsp red pepper flakes

½ cup (4 oz/125 g) sour cream

½ lb (250 g) rigatoni

2 pieces day-old bread such as baguette, coarse country, or sourdough, crusts removed, and cut into ½-inch (12-mm) cubes

---

Bring a medium pot of heavily salted water to a boil. Fill a large bowl with water and ice and set nearby. Add the kale to the boiling water and cook, stirring, for 1 minute. Using a slotted spoon, transfer to the ice bath. Once cool, drain and squeeze out any excess water. Set aside.

In a large sauté pan, warm the olive oil over medium heat. When the oil is hot, add the bell peppers and cook, stirring, until slightly softened, about 5 minutes. Add the onion and cook until the vegetables are softened and beginning to caramelize, about 6 minutes longer. Add the garlic and cook for another 30 seconds. Stir in the tomato paste and cook for about 2 minutes to allow it to darken. Add 1 tablespoon of the butter, the flour, and 1 teaspoon salt and stir to melt the butter and distribute the flour evenly. Cook for 3 minutes, stirring the whole time. Add the half-and-half and broth and bring to a simmer. Meanwhile, bring a large pot of water to a boil for the pasta.

When the sauce is just simmering, add the cheese, hot sauce, paprikas, and red pepper flakes. Reduce the heat slightly and stir until the cheese is melted. Add the sour cream and stir to combine. Taste and adjust the seasoning. Remove from the heat and keep warm.

Add a small handful of salt and the pasta to the boiling water and stir once. Cook until al dente, about 12 minutes or according to the package directions. While the pasta is cooking, in a frying pan, heat the remaining 1 tablespoon butter until foamy. Add the bread cubes and toast, stirring, until golden brown and crispy on all sides, about 5 minutes. Set aside.

Drain the pasta, transfer to a large bowl, add the sauce and kale, and toss to combine. Top with the croutons and serve right away.

MEATIFICATION Going on a meat-eating walkabout to figure out why in the world you're a vegetarian? Add oven-roasted chicken (kind of obvious right?).

DADDY NEEDS A SNACK

Daddy Needs a Snack Mr. Miyagi once said "Daniel-son anything can be a snack." We take that advice to heart. These aren't a "hold you over" snack like opening a bag of chips 'cause you're crashing hard and not gonna make it till dinner. These are classed-up, cocktail-party, art-opening, watching-the-game-from-the-VIP-box sort of snacks. Keep this chapter locked up in a safe and create a complex scavenger hunt to find it. Write a cryptic note saying, "open in case of snack emergency." Spill some coffee on the note and burn the edges to give it that old-time feel, like it came off a pirate ship from the wild west. Hide the note. Then get hypnotized to forget that you did that. One day you or your children will find the note, solve the hunt, and have the best snacks of all time.

If you feel inundated with cocktail talk involving multiple hard liquors, muddling, homemade bitters, and at-home oak-barrel aging, we feel your pain. It can be a little much. How hard do you really want to work just to have a drink? It's cool you figured out how to use Yelp and found that super-secret cocktail bar that everyone is talking about. But sometimes (often) you don't want to go out for a $14 cocktail. So if you've already got a few excellent liquor-driven cocktails in your arsenal, how about lightening things up with a few options that aren't so insanely boozy that right off the bat you'll be drunk texting your ex before the sun goes down.

MY DRINKS LIKE TO PARTY ALL THE TIME

"SMOOTH PUNCH" (by Rob Thomas & Carlos Sangria)

Sangria gets a bad rap as a drink that only old housewives sip on a bar's back deck during summer or it gets pegged as a girlie drink for people who can't get into liquor or beer. (Just FYI—those thoughts are ageist and sexist, respectively.) What we've crafted here is a bold fruit-forward punch that's more like a large-scale cocktail with fruit in it than sangria. The secret to sangria is that the fruit at the bottom soaks up all the booze. If the brains behind Dannon's fruit-on-the-bottom yogurt became a raging alcoholic, this is what it would resemble. Make sure you cut that fruit into bite-size chunks so people can have at it.

2 cups (16 fl oz/500 ml) dry red wine

1 cup (8 fl oz/250 ml) ruby port

1 cup (8 fl oz/250 ml) fresh lemonade

1 cup (8 fl oz/250 ml) Grand Marnier

2 peaches, pitted and chopped

1 cup (6 oz/185 g) diced cantaloupe

1 cup dark cherries, such as Morello or Michigan, pitted and halved

1 red apple, cored and chopped

1 organic orange, scrubbed but not peeled, chopped

Juice of 1 lemon

¼ tsp ground cinnamon

½ tsp ground cloves

¼ tsp ground ginger

2 qt (2 l) seltzer or club soda

SERVES 6–8

In a large pitcher, combine the red wine, port, lemonade, Grand Marnier, peaches, cantaloupe, cherries, apple, orange, lemon juice, cinnamon, cloves, and ginger. Stir well. Refrigerate until well chilled, at least 1 hour.

In individual glasses, mix 4 parts sangria to 1 part seltzer. Serve immediately.

It doesn't need to be perfect. What you're looking for is a bubbly drink with a light spritzer vibe without diluting the actual sangria. If you want to slow the getting–drunk process you can go 50–50 sangria to seltzer, though we suggest keeping it nice and boozy.

LILLET ALL DAY

Who doesn't want a cocktail that can be drunk ALL DAY LONG? It's like the little black dress of cocktails. This is a perfect drink to pair with a big hangover-cure meal because it's subtle and light and it's great for sipping on a rooftop or at a backyard get-together. It works anytime and it's not too heavy.

Ice

3 fl oz (90 ml) Lillet

1 fl oz (30 ml) fresh orange juice, plus orange peel for garnish (about ½ by 2 inches/12 mm by 5 cm)

3 dashes of orange bitters

Splash of tonic water

SERVES 1

Fill a rocks glass with ice water and let chill for at least 1 minute.

Fill a pint glass with ice. Pour in the Lillet, orange juice, and bitters and stir well.

Pour the ice water out of the rocks glass. Strain the drink into the glass. Top with the tonic water, garnish with the orange peel, and serve.

AMERICA 45

This cocktail is based on the French 75, which was named after a famous gun used during both world wars. Google it. We call ours the America 45, in homage to the American-made Colt. And in our version, you're not allowed to use Champagne or whatever they call it over there—only good old-fashioned American-made sparkling wine. America! Freedom! Alcohol! P.S. You are getting spied on.

Ice

2 fl oz (60 ml) gin

½ fl oz (15 ml) fresh lemon juice

½ fl oz simple syrup

½ cup (4 fl oz /125 ml) sparkling white wine, chilled

Candied ginger piece skewered on a toothpick for garnish (optional)

SERVES 1

Fill a Champagne glass with ice water and let chill for at least 1 minute.

Fill a cocktail shaker with ice. Pour in the gin, lemon juice, and simple syrup. Cover and shake vigorously for 15 seconds.

Pour the ice water out of the Champagne glass. Strain the drink into the glass and top with the sparkling wine. Garnish with the ginger skewer, if using, and serve.

2 Tbsp extra-virgin olive oil

2 tsp za'atar

½ tsp red pepper flakes

½ tsp hot paprika

½ tsp sesame seeds

Kosher salt

1 can (15½ oz/485 g) chickpeas, rinsed and drained

Finely grated zest of 1 lemon

SPICY, SALTY ROASTED CHICKPEAS

SERVES 4–6

Simplicity was the key here. Want the perfect bar snack? These are crunchy and salty and easy to pop in your mouth and wash down with a beer (or 10). We serve a version of them at Mile End Brooklyn all the time, and they are a big hit. Perhaps even worthy of the moniker "the Jell-O of bar snacks," there's always room for more of these little guys.

Preheat the oven to 375°F (190°C).

In a bowl, whisk together the olive oil, za'atar, red pepper flakes, paprika, sesame seeds, and ¼ teaspoon salt. Pat the chickpeas until they are very dry, then add them to the bowl and stir to coat well.

Spread the seasoned chickpeas in a single layer on a sheet tray and roast until crispy, about 30 minutes, stirring once part way through cooking.

Transfer the chickpeas to a bowl and toss in the lemon zest. Taste and adjust the seasoning. Serve right away. Store any leftover chickpeas in an airtight container at room temperature for up to 2 days; reheat them for 5 minutes in a 375°F (190°C) oven before serving.

CURRIED CHICKEN SALAD AND NAAN

SERVES 4

If the *Honey, I Shrunk the Kids* electromagnetic shrink ray was real, I'd be making delicious sandwiches and shrinking them down for snack-time consumption *on the reg*. Alas, that technology doesn't exist (and shrinking full sandwiches to bite-size portions is a poor allocation of both time and ingredients). So what we've done is apply this concept to a more realistic recipe. No electro-rays needed here—just an insanely flavorful chicken-in-a-bite that would make Wayne Szalinski proud. — Eli

Marinade

1 Tbsp extra-virgin olive oil

1 Tbsp fresh lime juice

1 Tbsp plain yogurt

2 shallots, minced

2 cloves garlic, smashed

1 Tbsp curry powder, preferably homemade (page 153)

2 Tbsp minced fresh cilantro stems

1 tsp kosher salt

1 lb (500 g) boneless, skinless chicken thighs

2 green onions, white and tender green parts only, trimmed and thinly sliced

½ cup (½ oz/15 g) packed fresh cilantro leaves, minced

6 Tbsp (3 oz/90 g) plain yogurt

1½ tsp curry powder, preferably homemade (page 153)

1 Tbsp fresh lime juice

2 naan, about 6 by 8 inches (15 by 20 cm)

To make the marinade, in a large bowl, combine the olive oil, lime juice, yogurt, shallots, garlic, curry powder, cilantro stems, and salt and stir to mix well.

Add the chicken to the marinade and turn to coat. Cover or seal tightly and refrigerate for at least 30 minutes or up to 1 day, stirring or turning occasionally.

Preheat the oven to 325°F (165°C).

Place the chicken, along with the marinade, on a sheet tray. Bake the chicken until opaque throughout, about 30 minutes. Remove from the oven and let cool completely. Leave the oven on.

While the chicken is cooling, in a large bowl, combine the green onions, cilantro leaves, yogurt, curry powder, and lime juice and stir to mix well. Finely chop the chicken, add to the bowl, and toss and stir to mix.

Put the naan on a sheet tray or directly on the oven rack and heat in the hot oven until warmed through, about 5 minutes.

To serve, cut the naan into roughly 2-inch (5-cm) pieces. Top each piece with about 1 tablespoon of the chicken salad, arranging the bites on a platter or individual plates as you work. Serve right away.

JAMÓN Y QUESO BITES WITH GAZPACHO CREAM

SERVES 8

I was on a huge gazpacho kick in the middle of the summer and we needed to finalize a menu for a private event we were catering. I was eating a big meat sandwich on a baguette (because that's how I roll daily) when mind and mouth and stomach joined together to create a cohesive appetizer idea. The *jamón y queso* bites would be tasty on their own, but the gazpacho *crema* is what takes this from being just "meat and cheese on bread" to being *muy delicioso pero peligroso. Imposible comer sólo una!* — Eli

Gazpacho Cream

½ cup (3 oz/90 g) chopped plum tomatoes

½ cup (2½ oz/75 g) seeded and diced, unpeeled English cucumber

2 Tbsp minced red onion

½ cup (2½ oz/75 g) diced red bell pepper

1 small clove garlic, minced

½ tsp smoked paprika

½ tsp kosher salt

¼ tsp cayenne pepper

¼ cup (2 oz/60 g) sour cream or crème fraîche

¼ cup (½ oz/15 g) sourdough bread pieces (crust removed)

1 baguette, cut into rounds ½ inch (12 mm) thick

¼ cup (2 fl oz/60 ml) olive oil

8 oz (250 g) Manchego cheese, thinly sliced

¼ lb (125 g) serrano ham, sliced paper-thin

To make the gazpacho cream, in a food processor, combine the tomatoes, cucumber, onion, bell pepper, garlic, paprika, salt, cayenne, sour cream, and bread pieces and process until smooth. Set aside.

Preheat the oven to 400°F (200°C).

Brush the baguette slices on both sides with the olive oil. Arrange on a sheet tray and toast in the oven for 5 minutes. Remove from the oven and top each baguette slice with the cheese, dividing it evenly. Return the pan to the oven and bake until the cheese is melted, about 3 minutes longer.

Remove from the oven and spoon about ½ teaspoon of the gazpacho cream on top of each cheese bite. Place a small slice of the ham on top of the cream, dividing the ham evenly among the bites. Serve right away.

8 oz (250 g) aged Cheddar cheese, shredded (about 2 cups)

3 Tbsp cream cheese

¼ cup (2 oz/60 g) minced roasted red pepper, homemade or jarred

1½ tsp smoked paprika

Kosher salt and freshly ground pepper

10–15 jalapeño peppers

1 cup (8 fl oz/250 ml) buttermilk

1 cup (5 oz/155 g) all-purpose flour

2 large eggs

1 cup (4 oz/125 g) panko bread crumbs

Vegetable oil for deep-frying

JALAPEÑO POPPERS

SERVES 8–10

If you already love jalapeño poppers, you might need to sit down when you try these for the first time. This recipe epitomizes what we love to do with our cookbooks: take something that is kinda good in theory but not really executed well and make it amazing. You've had the bowling-alley version and it's meh. And you've had the frozen version, which is wack. Now try making them from scratch and you'll understand why a little effort beforehand pays off huge once you get down to snacking. — **Max**

In a bowl, combine the Cheddar cheese, cream cheese, roasted pepper, paprika, ½ teaspoon salt, and a few cracks of black pepper.

Cut each jalapeño pepper in half lengthwise, but keep the halves near each other so you can reunite them when stuffed. Remove the seeds and membranes. (Disposable gloves are highly recommended for handling this many peppers.)

To stuff the peppers, take 1 jalapeño half and use a small spoon to fill it generously with the cheese mixture, filling it just over the edges. Place the other half on top and push down to make sure the cavity of both halves of the pepper are completely stuffed (the cheese mixture should ooze out slightly and help form a seal between the top and bottom halves). Repeat until you run out of cheese or peppers.

Set up a breading station by placing each of the following items in separate shallow bowls: the buttermilk; the flour; the eggs, beaten with 1 teaspoon water and 1 teaspoon salt; and the panko. Bread each stuffed jalapeño by carefully and completely covering it with each ingredient, in that exact order. Be sure to shake off the excess of each coating (or let it drip off) at each step, and coat the pepper completely with each ingredient before moving on to the next. Place the breaded jalapeños on a sheet tray as you work. When all of the peppers are breaded, refrigerate them to firm up while the oil heats.

Pour the oil to a depth of 4 inches (10 cm) into a deep pot or deep fryer and heat to 325°F (165°C) on a deep-frying thermometer. Add the poppers, a few at a time, to the hot oil, being careful not to crowd them in the pot. Fry until golden, about 5 minutes. Using a slotted spoon or a skimmer, transfer to paper towels to drain. Repeat to cook the remaining poppers, always letting the oil return to 325°F (165°C) between batches, if necessary.

Season the poppers lightly with salt while still warm. Let stand for 5 minutes to allow the cheese stuffing to cool slightly, then consume right away.

1 cup (8 fl oz/250 ml) warm water (about 100°F/38°C)

1 package (2½ tsp) active dry yeast

5 cups (25 oz/780 g) all-purpose flour

2 Tbsp light brown sugar

2 tsp kosher salt

⅓ cup (3 oz/90 g) unsalted butter, melted

1 Tbsp vegetable oil

1 large egg, lightly beaten

½ cup (3¾ oz/110 g) baking soda

¼ cup (2 oz/60 g) sea salt

⅓ cup (3 fl oz/80 ml) honey

1 cup (8 oz/250 g) brown mustard

PRETZEL BITES WITH HONEY MUSTARD

SERVES 8

Pretzels really had their glory days back in the 1980s, when teenagers had nothing to do except congregate in mall food courts and let the sexual tension flow. Unfortunately, as a "grown-up," you might want your pretzels to actually taste good instead of just be something to hold while you make awkward conversation about what bands you like. Once these pretzels emerge from the steamy oven, those angsty teen feelings you haven't experienced since the days at the mall will come rushing back. But instead of lusting over your ninth-grade crush, you'll be all hot and bothered for these salty bites.

In a small bowl, stir together the warm water and yeast and let stand until frothy, about 10 minutes.

Meanwhile, in a large bowl, whisk together the flour, sugar, and kosher salt. Slowly add the butter and stir to mix well. Add the yeast mixture, oil, and egg and stir with a wooden spoon until a rough dough comes together. Turn out onto a lightly floured work surface and knead until smooth and elastic, about 5 minutes. (See Challah, page 150, for detailed instructions on kneading.)

Place the dough in a clean, large, lightly oiled bowl and cover with a kitchen towel. Let the dough rise in a warm place until doubled in size, about 1 hour.

Position 1 rack in the center of the oven and a second rack in the lower third of the oven and preheat the oven to 450°F (230°C).

In a large pot, combine the baking soda with 8 cups (64 fl oz/2 l) water. Bring to a boil over high heat, stirring to dissolve the baking soda. Lightly spray 2 large sheet trays with cooking spray and set aside.

While the water is heating, punch down the dough and divide into 4 equal portions. Roll each portion into a rope about 1 inch (2.5 cm) in diameter, then cut each rope crosswise into 1-inch pieces.

Working in batches, add the dough pieces to the boiling water, a dozen or so at a time (don't crowd the pot), and cook for 30 seconds. Using a slotted spoon or skimmer, remove from the water, let drain, dab onto a kitchen towel to remove excess moisture, and then place on the prepared pan. Immediately sprinkle with some of the sea salt.

When all the pretzel bites are boiled and salted, transfer to the oven and bake for 5 minutes. Switch the pans between the racks and rotate them 180 degrees, then continue to bake until golden brown, about 5 minutes longer. Transfer to wire racks and let cool slightly.

In a small serving bowl, stir together the honey and mustard. Serve the pretzel bites warm with the honey mustard.

PISTACHIO-CORIANDER
SPIEDINI

SERVES 10–12

Rolled-up pieces of meat with delicious stuffing should be its own food group at the top of the pyramid. Unfortunately, the Surgeon General never returns our calls. The first time we ever really had amazing *spiedini* was at our friend Joe's popular Brooklyn restaurant Rucola. It's a must order whenever we go (as is the excellent pasta). When we were thinking of a cool meat technique to show you (pounding out the meat thinly) as part of a delicious dish perfect for dinner parties, we were lucky to find inspiration in that most satisfying appetizer.

2 lb (1 kg) sirloin, cut into slices ⅛ inch (3 mm) thick

1 cup (4 oz/125 g) salted roasted pistachios

½ cup (2 oz/60 g) panko bread crumbs

1 clove garlic, minced

Grated zest of 2 lemons

½ tsp ground coriander

½ tsp cayenne pepper

Juice of 1 lemon

Olive oil for brushing

Kosher salt

Working with 1 slice at a time, place the beef between 2 sheets of plastic wrap. On a clean work surface, using the flat side of a meat pounder or a small, heavy frying pan, pound out each slice to a thickness of about 2 credit cards. The goal is to get the meat extremely thin without tearing it. The slices should be about 2 inches (5 cm) by 4 inches (10 cm) after they are pounded. As you work, stack the slices in their plastic wrap to one side.

Put the pistachios in a food processor. Carefully pulse to process the nuts just to the consistency of a coarse meal (about the size of the panko) scraping down the sides of the bowl as needed. (Be careful not to overprocess, or the nuts will turn to butter.) Add the panko, garlic, lemon zest, coriander, and cayenne and pulse to blend. Add the lemon juice and purée until smooth.

Preheat the broiler.

Spread a thin layer of pistachio purée over each piece of meat. Carefully roll the meat up, taking care to keep the pistachio purée stuffed inside. Slide the rolled and stuffed sirloin pieces onto skewers. You should fill the equivalent of four 15-inch (38-cm) skewers.

Brush each skewer of meat with olive oil and lightly season with salt. Broil for 5–7 minutes, flipping halfway through. The spiedini are done when cooked to medium-rare inside. You may have to remove the smaller pieces from the oven earlier, as they will cook faster. Serve right away.

KABOCHA
SQUASH CROQUETTES

SERVES 4–6

Not all fried items are created equal. Did you have the friend in college who acquired a mini fryer and started to just fry everything in sight? Well, we did. And honestly some things are better left unfried. These are fried perfection: hot and flavorful insides with perfectly golden, crispy, crunchy outsides. If an older, more cultured version of Bart Simpson should encounter these, he just might say "nobody better lay a hand on my squash fritters."

1 kabocha squash

2 Tbsp extra-virgin olive oil

Kosher salt

2 Tbsp all-purpose flour, plus 1 cup (5 oz/155 g)

1 Tbsp peeled and minced fresh ginger

¼ tsp cayenne pepper

2 Tbsp thinly sliced fresh chives

3 large eggs

2 cups (8 oz/250 g) panko bread crumbs

Vegetable oil for deep-frying

Miso Aioli (page 152)

Preheat the oven to 350°F (180°C). Line 2 sheet trays with parchment paper.

Cut the squash in half. Scrape out the seeds and stringy membranes with a spoon. Brush the cut sides with the olive oil and sprinkle evenly with 1 teaspoon salt. Place the squash halves, cut side down, on a prepared sheet tray and bake until cooked tender, about 45 minutes.

Let the squash cool completely. Remove the skin and discard. Place the squash flesh in a food processor with the 2 tablespoons flour, the ginger, the cayenne, and salt to taste. Pulse to just combine, but do not over purée, then transfer to a bowl and fold in the chives. Using your hands, form the squash mixture into small balls about 1 inch (2.5 cm) in diameter, placing them on the second prepared sheet tray as you work.

Place the 1 cup (5 oz/155 g) flour in a large, shallow bowl. Break the eggs into another large shallow bowl and beat with 1 teaspoon salt and 2 tablespoons water. Put the bread crumbs in a third large, shallow bowl.

To bread each croquette, first coat it with the flour, shake off the excess flour, add to the eggs and roll to coat, let the excess egg drip off, and then toss well in the panko. As each croquette is coated, return it to the sheet tray. Refrigerate the croquettes while the oil heats.

Pour the oil to a depth of 3 inches (8 cm) into a deep pot or deep frier and heat to 350°F (180°C).

When the oil is ready, working in batches to avoid crowding the pan, carefully add the croquettes and fry until golden and crispy, 3–4 minutes. Using a slotted spoon or a skimmer, transfer the croquettes to paper towels to drain. Repeat with the remaining croquettes.

Arrange the croquettes on a platter and serve warm with the aioli.

2 large leeks, roots trimmed and top 1 inch (2.5 cm) removed, chopped, and thoroughly rinsed (about 2 cups/8 oz/250 g)

1½ cups (12 fl oz/375 ml) extra-virgin olive oil

Kosher salt

1 large head cauliflower, cored and broken into small florets

Juice of 3 lemons

Greek-style thick pita bread, cut into triangles and warmed in the oven

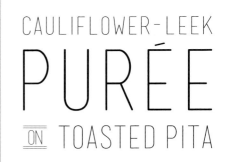

CAULIFLOWER-LEEK
PURÉE
ON TOASTED PITA

SERVES 6–8

This recipe came about while we were looking for an alternative to hummus or baba ghanoush. We had a lot of cauliflower in-house, so by roasting and puréeing it until silky smooth, we were able to achieve a delicious but distinctly different spread. We recommend serving this with Marash pepper sprinkled over the top. If you can't find that, smoked paprika works well. We made this at a fashion event and people came back for more five times. Moral of the story: it's delicious and people in fashion actually eat. Who knew? — Eli

Preheat the oven to 450°F (230°C).

Spin or pat the leeks dry. In a large bowl, combine the leeks with ¼ cup (2 fl oz/60 ml) of the olive oil and 1 teaspoon salt and toss to coat well. Spread in a single layer on one-half of a large sheet tray.

In the same bowl, toss the cauliflower with another ¼ cup of the olive oil and 1 teaspoon salt. Spread on the other half of the same sheet tray.

Transfer the sheet tray to the oven and roast until the leek pieces start to char around the edges but are still green, about 20 minutes. Remove the pan from the oven and transfer the leeks to a bowl. Discard any pieces that are completely blackened, but some burnt edges will contribute flavor, so keep those.

Return the pan to the oven and roast the cauliflower until deep golden brown but not black or burned, 15–20 minutes longer. As the batch roasts, peek once in a while and transfer any florets that reach a deep gold to a separate bowl from the leeks. When all of the cauliflower is done, remove the pan from the oven and add the remaining cauliflower to the bowl.

Place half of the cauliflower and half of the leeks in a blender (or food processor, although it won't get as smooth and silky in a food processor) and add ½ cup (4 fl oz/125 ml) of the olive oil and all of the lemon juice. Blend on low speed briefly or pulse a few times to mix, then gradually raise the blender speed to high or use longer pulses with the food processor until the mixture is a smooth purée, 1–2 minutes.

With the machine running, add the remaining cauliflower and leeks and the remaining ½ cup olive oil and process until smooth. If the purée seems stiff or needs help blending, add up to ¼ cup (2 fl oz/60 ml) water, 1 teaspoon at a time. Turn off the machine and scrape down the sides of the blender jar as needed to ensure even blending.

Taste and adjust the seasoning with more salt or lemon juice, if necessary. Serve warm or at room temperature with the pita, or let cool completely and store in an airtight container in the refrigerator for up to 1 week. Bring to room temperature before serving.

Juice of 3 limes (about 6 Tbsp/ 3 fl oz/90 ml)

3 Tbsp extra-virgin olive oil

½ lb (250 g) sushi-grade hamachi, fluke, or mahi mahi, cut into pieces about 1 inch (2.5 cm) long and ⅛ inch (3 mm) thick

1 ripe avocado, pitted, peeled, and cut into pieces similar in size to the fish

¼ cup (⅓ oz/10 g) minced fresh cilantro stems

3 red Fresno peppers, thinly sliced

½ cup (2 oz/60 g) crushed pita or tortilla chips for serving

In a bowl, whisk together the lime juice and olive oil until well blended. Add the fish and avocado and stir to coat thoroughly. Gently fold in the cilantro stems and peppers. Let stand at room temperature for 15 minutes.

Taste and adjust the seasoning and finish with a drizzle of olive oil. Serve with the pita chips.

CEVICHE

SERVES 4–6

Ceviche can scare people, since many believe raw fish only belongs in the domain of those with extensive culinary skill and seafood backgrounds. But in truth, ceviche is insanely easy to make, as it's much harder to cook fish than to "pickle" it, which is essentially what you are doing here. Buy the highest-quality fish possible, keep it cold until you're ready to use it, and serve the ceviche immediately once it's ready. Follow these steps and you'll be transported to a magical place where "La Isla Bonita" plays on repeat, there's a mojito lazy river, and if you snap your fingers, a chimpanzee in a tuxedo brings you a banana split for dessert. — **Max**

COD FRITTERS ON TOSTADAS

Vegetable oil for deep-frying

½ lb (250 g) boneless, skinless cod, hake, or pollock fillets

1 cup (1 oz/30 g) packed fresh flat-leaf parsley leaves, finely chopped

½ cup (2 oz/60 g) panko bread crumbs

⅓ cup (2 oz/60 g) minced yellow onion

3 Tbsp heavy cream

Grated zest and juice of 1 lemon

1 large egg, beaten

1 Tbsp mustard seeds, toasted

Kosher salt

½ tsp red pepper flakes

½ tsp fish sauce

Five corn tortillas or store-bought tostadas, each 6 inches (15 cm) in diameter

Mexican crema, sour cream, or crème fraîche for garnish

Smoked paprika for dusting

SERVES 4–6

This recipe might seem hard, but basically it's just chopping and frying, which are two things we know you've done before. So don't let the cod scare you. Be like Indiana Jones in the *Last Crusade* and take that walk of faith right into the deep fryer. A note from our lawyers: The cod, not you, should go into the deep fryer. The walk of faith is metaphorical to represent you overcoming your culinary fears. — **Max**

Pour the oil to a depth of 2 inches (5 cm) into a deep pot or deep fryer and heat to 350°F (180°C).

While the oil is heating, make the fritter batter: Mince the fish with a sharp chef's knife or in a food processor. (The fish should have an almost pastelike texture. If it's too coarse, the balls won't hold together.) In a large bowl, combine the fish, parsley, bread crumbs, onion, cream, lemon zest and juice, egg, mustard seeds, 1 teaspoon salt, red pepper flakes, and fish sauce and stir to mix well. Using your hands, form the fish mixture into small balls about 1 inch (2.5 cm) in diameter, placing them on a sheet tray as you work.

When the oil is ready, if frying your own tostadas, carefully lower 1 or 2 tortillas into the oil and fry, flipping them once halfway through, until the bubbles subside, 1–2 minutes. Using tongs or a skimmer, transfer to paper towels to drain, then sprinkle lightly with salt while still warm. Repeat with the remaining tortillas, always letting the oil return to 350°F (180°C) before adding more tortillas.

When all of the tortillas have been fried, begin adding the fritters to the hot oil, a few at a time, being careful not to crowd the pan. Fry until cooked through and golden brown, about 2 minutes. Using the skimmer or a slotted spoon, transfer to paper towels to drain. Repeat with the remaining fritters, always letting the oil return to 350°F (180°C) before adding the next batch.

To serve, crack the tostadas into quarters. Place a small dollop of the crema on each tostada piece, then a fritter, arranging the bites on a serving platter as you work. Dust lightly with the paprika. Serve right away.

TASTY CHOICES BEFORE TASTELESS DECISIONS

Tasty Choices before Tasteless Decisions

There are a multitude of bad decisions that can be made in an evening. But the evening can always start off right. Look, we aren't your parents or the police, but we can tell you to hold on to your wallet, always call for a ride, and never go to the bathroom on the street under any circumstances. Where we can advise you as experts is the best way to kick off your night right. No one wants to arrive at a bowling birthday party, a hot date, or a rave feeling lethargic and weighed down. You want to be ready to bowl a 300, score big-time, and dance until the sun comes up. These recipes are the anti-bacon mac and cheese. Cook easy and start light. Then, go hard and party heavy.

WHEAT BERRY SALAD

WITH STRAWBERRIES AND CRISPY SHALLOTS

1 cup (7 oz/220 g) wheat berries

Kosher salt

2 cups (16 fl oz/500 ml) vegetable oil

2 shallots, cut into slices about ⅛ inch (3 mm) thick

2 cups (8 oz/250 g) strawberries, stemmed and quartered if large or halved if small

3 Tbsp cider vinegar

2 tsp brown sugar

¼ tsp finely chopped fresh rosemary

3 Tbsp extra-virgin olive oil

¼ cup (1 oz/30 g) shredded Parmesan cheese

½ cup (¾ oz/20 g) finely chopped fresh flat-leaf parsley

SERVES 4

This started as a rye berry salad, but since none of our friends could find them, we now have a wheat berry salad. If you don't have a CSA, didn't go to a small liberal arts college, or don't wear Birkenstocks, you probably wouldn't know the difference anyways. Ignorance is sometimes bliss. It doesn't matter if you're heading out to a poetry slam or you're seeing Stone Roses in concert, this salad is a light way to start your heavy evening.

In a saucepan, combine the wheat berries and 4 cups (32 fl oz/1 l) water and bring to a boil over high heat. Reduce the heat to low and simmer for 30 minutes. Add a pinch of salt and continue to simmer until tender, about 15 more minutes.

Meanwhile, in a medium saucepan, heat the vegetable oil to 300°F (150°C). When the oil is hot, add the sliced shallots. Be careful not to splash hot oil on yourself; use a skimmer or slotted spoon to lower them in, if you like. Work in batches if needed to avoid crowding the pan. Slowly fry the shallots until they are crispy and golden and the bubbles subside, about 15 minutes. Be careful not to let them burn. Using the skimmer, transfer to paper towels to drain. Season lightly with salt while still warm.

While the shallots are frying, put the strawberries in a bowl and add 1 tablespoon of the vinegar, the brown sugar, the rosemary, and ¼ teaspoon salt. Toss to combine and let macerate at room temperature for at least 15 minutes.

When the wheat berries are done, drain in a colander set in the sink and rinse under cold running water, then drain again thoroughly. Transfer to a large serving bowl.

To assemble, in a small bowl, whisk together the olive oil, the remaining 2 tablespoons vinegar, the cheese, and ¼ teaspoon salt. Add half of the strawberries and half of the parsley to the bowl with the wheat berries. Pour in the vinaigrette and toss gently to mix well. Taste and adjust the seasoning. Top with the remaining strawberries and parsley and the crispy shallots. Serve right away.

2 Tbsp extra-virgin olive oil

1 yellow onion, minced

2 cloves garlic, minced

2 lb (1 kg) mussels, scrubbed, debearded, and rinsed

1 cup (8 fl oz/250 ml) saison or other Belgian farmhouse ale

1 tsp saffron threads

½ tsp cayenne pepper

Kosher salt and freshly ground pepper

1 Tbsp unsalted butter

¼ cup (2 fl oz/60 ml) sherry vinegar

½ cup (¾ oz/20 g) chopped fresh flat-leaf parsley leaves

Crusty bread for serving

MUSSELS WITH SAFFRON AND BEER

SERVES 2

"Mussels and saffron" sounds like the title of a bad rom-com movie from the 1980s about two lost souls traveling abroad that meet in Belgium on a cold rainy night and share dreams for their futures over a classic bowl of *moules frites*. Randomly reconnecting twenty years later over a bowl of saffron mussels, they kiss, realizing they've been missing each other all along. Doesn't this movie sound like it sucks? Don't wait 20 years to realize that you've been missing this recipe all along.

In a large, heavy-bottomed sauté pan with tall sides or rondeau with a tight-fitting lid, heat the olive oil over medium heat. When the oil is hot, add the onion and sauté until lightly browned, about 5 minutes. Add the garlic and sauté for 1 minute.

Add the mussels, discarding any that do not close to the touch, and stir for 1 minute. Add the ale to the pan, then stir in the saffron, cayenne, and a pinch each of salt and black pepper and cover immediately. Raise the heat to medium high, bring to a brisk simmer, and cook until the mussels have opened, 4–6 minutes. Discard any mussels that fail to open.

Using a slotted spoon, transfer the mussels to a large serving bowl and cover with a plate to keep warm. Add the butter, vinegar, and a pinch of salt to the pan juices and return to a simmer. Cook until fragrant and slightly thickened, 4–6 minutes. Return the mussels to the pot and remove from the heat. Sprinkle the parsley over the top and serve right away with crusty bread.

SEARED TUNA SALAD
WITH PICKLED DAIKON AND MISO VINAIGRETTE

SERVES 2

We're not really sure what decade this salad is from. Something about it seems really 1980s, like what ladies ate when they got sick of chicken Caesar and discovered "Asian food." But then it also seems super 1990s, like Wall Street guys taking power lunches after their doctor told them not to eat red meat anymore. Obviously we know nothing about salad history, but we do know that this salad is delicious. Gordon Gekko, Carrie Bradshaw—everyone loves salad.

Pickled Vegetables

1 daikon radish, cut into slices ¼ inch (6 mm) thick

1 carrot, peeled and cut into slices ¼ inch (6 mm) thick

½ red onion, cut into julienne

½ cup (4 fl oz/125 ml) rice vinegar

2 Tbsp sugar

2 tsp kosher salt

Miso Vinaigrette

2 Tbsp rice vinegar

1 Tbsp toasted sesame oil

1 Tbsp white miso

1 tsp soy sauce

2 Tbsp extra-virgin olive oil

6 oz (185 g) sashimi-grade tuna loin

Kosher salt

2 bunches green onions, white and tender green parts only, trimmed and cut into pieces about 3 inches (7.5 m) long

2 cups (2 oz/60 g) baby arugula

To make the pickled vegetables, put the radish, carrot, and onion in a small heatproof bowl. In a small saucepan, combine the vinegar, sugar, salt, and 1 cup (8 fl oz/250 ml) water and bring to a simmer over medium-high heat. Stir until the sugar and salt dissolve. Pour the pickling liquid over the vegetables. Let stand at room temperature for at least 2 hours or preferably refrigerate overnight.

When you're ready to serve, make the miso vinaigrette. In a small bowl, whisk together the rice vinegar, the sesame oil, the miso, and the soy sauce. Set aside.

Heat the olive oil in a frying pan over high heat until hot but not smoking. Season the tuna on both sides with salt. Place the tuna in the hot oil and sear on each side for 15 seconds. Transfer the tuna to a cutting board. Add the green onions to the hot pan and sauté until blistered and soft, about 2 minutes. Remove from the heat.

To serve, drain the pickled vegetables and toss in a large bowl with the arugula and half of the vinaigrette. Carve the tuna against the grain into slices about ¼ inch (6 mm) thick. Place half of the salad on each serving plate and arrange the tuna and green onions over the top. Drizzle the remaining vinaigrette over the tuna and serve right away.

1 whole chicken, about 3 lb (1.5 kg)

2 Tbsp dried oregano

2 tsp sweet paprika

½ tsp hot paprika

½ tsp cayenne pepper

2 tsp granulated onion

½ tsp granulated garlic

Kosher salt and freshly ground pepper

2 Tbsp extra-virgin olive oil

1 shallot, minced

1 clove garlic, minced

½ jalapeño pepper, seeded and minced

Leaves from 1 bunch Swiss chard, stems and spines removed

1 lemon, halved

PAN-ROASTED CAJUN CHICKEN
OVER WILTED GREENS

SERVES 4–6

Pressing a chicken is the ultimate basic technique that you can keep using forever to cook a whole chicken perfectly. Most people looking for a healthy recipe would go for a boneless chicken breast. I'm sorry, but this just isn't that kind of cookbook, okay? Live a little. Eat the crispy skin. — **Max**

Preheat the oven to 425°F (220°C).

First, using kitchen shears, cut the back out of the chicken. Beginning at the bottom, use the shears to slice on the right side of the backbone, between the thigh bone and the backbone. Continue up the chicken, keeping close to the backbone until separated completely along one side. Repeat on the left side, starting on the other side of the backbone, which is about 1½ inches (4 cm) wide. Remove and discard the backbone then trim any excess bones sticking out of the bird. Press the chicken flat on the cutting board, skin side up.

In a small bowl, stir together the oregano, the two paprikas, cayenne, granulated onion and garlic, 1 teaspoon salt, and 2 teaspoons black pepper. Season the chicken on all sides with the spice mix, rubbing it in thoroughly.

In a large ovenproof frying pan, warm the olive oil over medium-high heat. When the oil is hot, place the chicken, skin side down, in the pan. Using the back of your hand, press down on the chicken to bring the skin in contact with the oil and cook until the skin is evenly and deeply caramelized, about 5 minutes. Rotate the chicken occasionally to ensure all areas are heating evenly. Transfer the pan to the oven and roast for 10 minutes. Turn the bird skin side up and roast for 10 minutes longer. When the chicken is almost done (an instant-read thermometer inserted into the thickest part should register 120°–130°F/49°–55°C), turn it skin side down and roast until the thermometer registers 155°–160°F (68°–71°C). The total time in the oven should be 30–45 minutes, depending on the size of the chicken. Transfer the chicken, skin side up, to a cutting board, and let rest for at least 10 minutes.

Pour off all but 2 tablespoons of the fat from the pan and place the pan over medium heat. Add the shallot, garlic, and jalapeño and sauté until softened and starting to brown, about 2 minutes. Add the chard and cook, stirring, just until evenly wilted, about 3 minutes. Remove from the heat and keep warm.

Carve the chicken into 8 pieces: 4 breast pieces, 2 thighs, and 2 drumsticks. Squeeze the lemon halves over the greens and chicken, then pile the greens on a platter and arrange the chicken on top. Serve right away.

SOBA
NOODLES WITH
SHIITAKE MUSHROOMS
AND RADISH

SERVES 2–4

As much as everyone loves the occasional so-so Chinese food delivered right to the door, often it's much more fulfilling and significantly less gross to make dinner yourself. If it's Sunday and you're about to binge out on food (and AMC), we understand. Put on your pj's, earmark this recipe, and move on to a different chapter. But if you've got plans later and don't want to be weighted down, this recipe is light and quick and the poaching liquid doubles as your sauce, so that's one less pan to clean up.

3 Tbsp soy sauce

2 Tbsp rice vinegar

1 Tbsp mirin

1 Tbsp Sriracha

2 boneless, skinless chicken thighs, thinly sliced

½ lb (8 oz/250 g) soba noodles

Kosher salt

2 Tbsp olive oil

¼ lb (4 oz/125 g) shiitake mushrooms, stemmed

1 bunch green onions, white and tender green parts only, trimmed and thinly sliced

2 Tbsp toasted sesame oil

2 radishes, grated

In a small saucepan, combine the soy sauce, vinegar, mirin, Sriracha, and 3 tablespoons water and bring to a simmer over high heat. Reduce the heat to medium-low and add the chicken. Simmer gently until the chicken is opaque throughout, about 10 minutes. The liquid will thicken slightly as the chicken cooks, but add a bit more water if it gets dry.

Meanwhile, bring a pot of water to a boil over high heat. Add the soba noodles and a pinch of salt, and cook until al dente, about 5 minutes or according to the package directions. Immediately drain in a colander set in the sink, rinse under cold running water, and let drain again thoroughly.

In a sauté pan, heat the olive oil over high heat. When the oil is hot, add the mushrooms and a pinch of salt and cook, stirring often, until tender, 2–3 minutes.

In a bowl, toss the soba noodles with the warm chicken and sauce, warm mushrooms, and half of the green onions. Transfer to a serving bowl and top with the remaining green onions, sesame oil, and radish. Serve right away.

2 lb (1 kg) carrots, peeled

½ cup (4 fl oz/125 ml) olive oil, plus extra for drizzling

½ cup (4 fl oz/125 ml) rice vinegar

1 Tbsp toasted sesame oil

2 tsp mirin

3 Tbsp peeled and coarsely chopped fresh ginger

2 Tbsp wasabi paste

Kosher salt

¼ lb (125 g) sugar snap peas, thinly sliced lengthwise

2 tablespoons black sesame seeds

1 sheet nori seaweed, cut into matchsticks

CARROT-WASABI SOUP

SERVES 4

Preheat the oven to 375°F (190°C).

Split the carrots lengthwise and then cut crosswise into 1-inch (2.5-cm) pieces. Put the carrots in a bowl and toss with ¼ cup (2 fl oz/60 ml) of the olive oil. Spread in a single layer on a sheet tray and roast until softened but not starting to brown, about 15 minutes.

Transfer the carrots to a blender or food processor and add the remaining ¼ cup olive oil. With the machine running, add 2 cups (16 fl oz/500 ml) water, ½ cup (4 fl oz/125 ml) at a time, and process until the mixture is smooth, about 3 minutes. (The mixture will get smoother in a blender than a food processor, but you may have to work in batches.) Add the vinegar, sesame oil, mirin, ginger, wasabi, and 1 tsp salt and process for 1 minute. Taste and adjust the seasoning.

Transfer the soup to a bowl or pitcher, cover and refrigerate until well chilled, at least 2 hours. To serve, ladle or pour the soup into individual bowls, dividing it evenly, and garnish each serving with the snap peas, sesame seeds, seaweed, and a drizzle of olive oil. Serve right away.

I could write something here about how this soup was influenced by this amazing trip where I ate my way across Southeast Asia and my vision on soup was forever changed, but to be honest I just had a lot of carrots lying around. We suggest serving this soup cold, but it would be great hot in winter. Definitely use a blender, so it's the silkiest, smoothest texture it can possibly be, and use lots of garnish so that each bite has a variety of textures. Fun! — Eli

FENNEL SALAD WITH CANDIED PUMPKIN SEEDS AND HEARTS OF PALM

SERVES 2–4

This salad has some intense ingredients. Fennel and radish don't usually rank high as favorite vegetables. But the candied pumpkin seeds (which you may have made at summer camp, or with your family around Halloween) are really the jammy jam. Sweet and crunchy. If we were douches, we'd say something about these being the umami in the salad but we are not so we won't.

Spiced Pumpkin Seeds

1 cup (4 oz/125 g) hulled pumpkin seeds

½ tsp hot paprika

¼ tsp ground coriander

Pinch of cayenne pepper

Pinch of freshly ground pepper

Pinch of kosher salt

¼ cup (2 oz/60 g) sugar

2 large fennel bulbs, trimmed and cored, about 2 Tbsp fronds reserved for garnish

1 bunch red radishes, trimmed

2 cans (15 oz/470 g each) hearts of palm, drained and cut into slices ¼ inch (6 mm) thick

Leaves of 4 fresh mint sprigs, roughly chopped

Leaves of 4 fresh marjoram sprigs, roughly chopped

⅓ cup (3 fl oz/90 ml) fresh grapefruit juice

3 Tbsp extra-virgin olive oil

2 Tbsp cider vinegar

To make the spiced pumpkin seeds, preheat the oven to 350°F (180°C). Line a sheet tray with parchment paper and coat the paper lightly with cooking spray. Have ready a second sheet tray.

Spread the pumpkin seeds on the unlined sheet tray and bake, stirring once or twice, until lightly browned and toasty smelling, about 5 minutes. Meanwhile, in a small bowl, whisk together the paprika, coriander, cayenne, black pepper, and salt.

Sprinkle the sugar in a large frying pan and place over high heat. Stir to help the sugar melt. When it starts to caramelize and brown, after 30–60 seconds, add the pumpkin seeds and spice mixture and toss well. Leave over high heat while you quickly stir to make sure all the seeds are equally coated. Pour the seeds on the parchment-lined pan, spread them out in a single layer, and let cool completely.

Using a mandoline or a sharp chef's knife, shave or slice the fennel bulbs thinly (about the thickness of 2 credit cards) and put in a large bowl. Shave or slice the radishes and add to the same bowl. Add the hearts of palm, mint, and marjoram and toss to distribute all of the ingredients evenly.

In a small bowl, whisk together the grapefruit juice, olive oil, and vinegar. Pour the vinaigrette over the salad and toss to coat well. Add the pumpkin seeds and toss. Garnish with the reserved fronds and serve right away. (If you are going to transport the salad or are serving later, reserve the pumpkin seeds and toss in right before serving.)

JUSTBECAUSE YOUDONTHAVE FRIENDSDOESNT MEANYOUCANT MAKEDINNER

Just Because You Don't Have Friends Doesn't Mean You Can't Make Dinner

You've texted everyone and it's just not happening tonight. They're either "tired" or "just taking it easy." You feel like there's a conspiracy and they are all at some new amazingly fun bar together, without you. That can't be happening though, right? News flash—that's what's actually happening. Your friends collectively decided that you're not in the group anymore. And it's not them. It's definitely you. So yeah, you're gonna have to learn to deal with that and may need to talk to a professional. But tonight? Fuck 'em. You've got yourself and that's all you need. Well you and a pile of steak nachos and the *Blade Runner* director's cut. Some of these portions are huge, but you just got dumped by ALL your friends. So cook up a ree-dick amount of food and melt into your couch. Actually, can we come over?

3 Tbsp extra-virgin olive oil, or more if needed

¼ cup (1½ oz/45 g) minced yellow onion

½-inch (12-mm) piece fresh ginger, peeled and minced

1 clove garlic, minced

5 oz (155 g) baby spinach

¼ tsp ground cumin

⅛ tsp ground coriander

1 Tbsp unsalted butter, at room temperature

10–15 fresh mint leaves

1 small zucchini, trimmed and cut into 1-inch (2.5-cm) pieces

Kosher salt

4 oz (125 g) halloumi cheese, cut into slices about ½ inch (12 mm) thick

SEARED HALLOUMI WITH SPINACH AND ZUCCHINI

SERVES 1

In a saucepan, heat 2 tablespoons of the olive oil over low heat. Add the onion, ginger, and garlic and sauté until softened and translucent, about 10 minutes. Add the spinach, cumin, and coriander, raise the heat to medium, and cook until the spinach is just wilted, about 2 minutes. Fold in the butter and mint leaves. Remove from the heat and set aside.

In a large sauté pan, heat the remaining 1 tablespoon olive oil over medium-high heat. Carefully place the zucchini chunks in the pan so they are not touching and season with salt. Cook until golden on the first side, about 3 minutes, then turn them over to brown on the second side. When you turn the zucchini, move them closer together to make room in the pan for the halloumi slices. (Use a second pan if it's too crowded.) Add the cheese slices and a little more oil if the pan seems dry. After 2 minutes, turn the halloumi over. When all of the zucchini and halloumi slices are nicely browned on both sides, remove from the heat.

To serve, place the spinach mixture on a plate. Arrange the zucchini and halloumi slices on top. Serve right away.

Halloumi is cheese that you can fry in a pan. It melts but only a little, so it keeps its shape and gets a beautiful golden crust. Nonmelting cheese is so counterintuitive and wondrous that you probably think that some kind of modern scientist must have invented it in the same place he invented bubble tea, Dippin' Dots, Cheez Whiz, and that chocolate syrup that gets hard when it cools. But really, it was Mother Nature. Or maybe it was her really quiet son Steve who was always out back in the garden. Can't remember.

FALAFEL BURGER

MAKES UP TO 4 BURGERS

We both love burgers as much as life itself, but honestly there is a time when a veggie burger is called for. And that's when you have nothing else in your fridge and you're starving and broke and have no one to turn to and then you see that can of chickpeas in your pantry that you've been putting off using until now. Fear not, for that's exactly what this recipe is for. Make a burger and cheer the hell up for tomorrow will be a new day filled with meaty options. Freeze the leftovers for an easy snack when you reach that dark grocery-free place again.

1 small eggplant, trimmed and cut crosswise into slices ¼ inch (6 mm) thick

3 Tbsp extra-virgin olive oil

Kosher salt

Burgers

1 can (15½ oz/485 g) chickpeas, rinsed and drained

1 cup (5 oz/155 g) pecans, lightly toasted

1 cup (1 oz/30 g) fresh flat-leaf parsley leaves, finely chopped

Juice of 1 lemon

5 Tbsp (3 fl oz/80 ml) extra-virgin olive oil, or more if needed

1 large egg, beaten

1 tsp hot paprika

1 tsp fennel powder

½ tsp cardamom

1 tsp dried oregano

1 tsp ground allspice

¼ tsp ground coriander

Kosher salt and freshly ground pepper

¼ cup (2 fl oz/60 ml) good-quality mayonnaise

2 Tbsp Sriracha, or more to taste

Shredded lettuce, for serving

Whole-wheat buns, split and toasted

Preheat the oven to 375°F (190°C). Arrange the eggplant slices on a sheet pan. Drizzle with the olive oil, sprinkle generously with salt, and toss to coat. Roast until golden brown, about 20 minutes.

While the eggplant is roasting, make the burgers. In a food processor, purée the chickpeas until nearly smooth. A few small chunks are okay. Transfer to a large bowl.

Add the pecans, parsley, lemon juice, 1 tablespoon of the olive oil, the egg, paprika, fennel, cardamom, oregano, allspice, coriander, 1 teaspoon salt, and ½ teaspoon pepper to the bowl and mix together with your hands. Add a splash of water if the mixture is dry. Let stand at room temperature for 10 minutes.

In a nonstick frying pan, heat the remaining 4 tablespoons (2 fl oz/60 ml) olive oil over medium heat. While the oil is heating, shape about one-fourth of the burger mixture into a patty about 1 inch (2.5 cm) thick. When the oil is hot, place the patty in the pan and cook until deep golden brown on the first side, about 3 minutes. Flip over, press down lightly to even it out, and cook until the second side is deeply browned, the edges are crispy, and the center is hot, about 3 minutes longer. Repeat to cook more patties as you like, adding more oil to the pan if it is dry. (Leftover patties should be cooked within 1 day; refrigerate uneaten cooked patties well wrapped in plastic wrap for up to 3 days or freeze for up to 2 weeks).

In a bowl, stir together the mayo and the Sriracha. For each burger, put a smear of spicy mayo on the bottom half of a bun, top with some lettuce, then the burger, and finally the eggplant. Serve right away.

¼ cup (1¾ oz/50 g) dried cannellini beans, picked over for stones or grit

Kosher salt

4 Tbsp (2 fl oz/60 ml) extra-virgin olive oil

1 small yellow onion, cut into julienne

1 clove garlic, minced

1 plum tomato, cored and cut into ½-inch (12-mm) dice

1 cup (8 fl oz/250 ml) dry white wine

A few fresh basil sprigs, plus more for garnish

6 littleneck clams, scrubbed

1 skin-on striped bass fillet, about 4 oz (125 g)

A pinch of red pepper flakes

STRIPED BASS
WITH CLAMS
AND WHITE BEANS

SERVES 1

Some might say this is a classy "date night" kind of recipe. And those people wouldn't necessarily be wrong. You can cook this for you and your boo and be set for the night. But just 'cause you don't have a special someone doesn't mean you can't cook up a perfect piece of fish for yourself. Light a candle and crank up the Luther Vandross. You deserve it. If you're using a thick fillet here, it might need a minute or two in a preheated 350°F (180°C) oven to finish.

In a bowl, soak the beans in water to cover overnight. Drain, rinse, and drain again. In a saucepan, combine the beans with water to cover, bring to a boil, reduce the heat to a simmer, and cook, adding 1 tablespoon salt after about 30 minutes, until tender, about 45 minutes. Drain and set aside.

In a large frying pan, warm 2 tablespoons of the olive oil over medium heat. Add the onion and sauté until softened and lightly browned, 5–7 minutes. Add the garlic and cook for 1 minute. Add the tomato and sauté until softened, about 3 minutes. Add the wine and basil, bring to a simmer, and then add the clams, discarding any that do not close to the touch. Cover tightly and cook, shaking the pan every minute or so, until the clams have opened, about 10 minutes. As the clams open, transfer them to a bowl. Remove the pan from the heat and discard any clams that failed to open and the basil; reserve the pan juices. Pull the clams from their shells, chop coarsely, and reserve.

Pat the fish dry and season lightly on both sides with salt. In a clean frying pan, heat the remaining 2 tablespoons olive oil over medium heat. When the oil is hot, add the fillet, skin side down, and press lightly with a spatula to bring the skin in contact with the oil. After 30 seconds or so, when you will feel the flesh relax, remove the spatula and continue cooking for about 2 minutes. Check the underside of the fish; if the skin has not begun to brown, press on the fish again; this will help yield the perfect crispy skin. When the skin is browned and crisp and the two-thirds of the thickness of the flesh is opaque, reduce the heat to medium-low, flip the fillet, and cook until opaque throughout, about 2 minutes longer. Transfer the fillet, skin side up, to paper towels to drain.

Meanwhile, add the clams, red pepper flakes, and beans to the reserved pan juices and bring to a simmer. Taste and adjust the seasoning. To serve, place the bean sauce in a shallow bowl and top with the fillet, skin side up.

SAUSAGE AND PEPPER RICE PILAF

SERVES 1, PLUS LOTS OF LEFTOVERS FOR LUNCH

Rice pilaf is one of those things that our mom used to make all the time. I thought it was awesome and couldn't figure out how all the flavors got in there. Then I started cooking and found the Near East brand boxes in the pantry, and it was like when I realized that the tooth fairy wasn't real. Lines were crossed. Trust was broken. Things changed and they never went back. It was really that day that I think my childhood ended. Anyways, hope you enjoy this recipe! — **Max**

3 Tbsp extra-virgin olive oil

1 link spicy Italian sausage, casing removed and broken into 1-inch (2.5-cm) pieces

½ small yellow onion, minced

½ green bell pepper, seeded and minced

1 rib celery, minced

1 clove garlic, minced

1 plum tomato, cut into ½-inch (12-mm) dice

1 Tbsp tomato paste

1 cup (7 oz/220 g) jasmine rice, rinsed and drained

1⅓ cups (10½ fl oz/330 ml) chicken stock

Kosher salt and freshly ground pepper

Cayenne pepper

¼ tsp hot paprika

¼ cup (1¼ oz/37 g) slivered blanched almonds, toasted

In a saucepan, heat 1 tablespoon of the olive oil over high heat. Add the sausage and fry quickly until nicely browned on all sides, about 2 minutes. (It's okay if it is still raw inside.) Transfer to a plate and set aside.

Reduce the heat to medium and add the remaining 2 tablespoons olive oil. Add the onion, bell pepper, and celery and sauté until softened, about 5 minutes. Add the garlic and diced tomato and sauté for 2 minutes. Add the tomato paste and rice and stir until the tomato paste is evenly distributed, about 2 minutes.

Stir in the chicken stock, ½ teaspoon salt, a pinch each of black pepper and cayenne, and the hot paprika and return the sausage to the pan. Bring to a simmer, then reduce the heat to low, cover, and cook for about 12 minutes. Remove from the heat and let stand, covered, for 10 minutes without uncovering.

Place the desired amount in a bowl, garnish with the toasted almonds, and serve immediately. (The rice will keep, tightly covered in the fridge, for up to 4 days.)

Salsa

1 jalapeño pepper, finely diced

1 Fresno pepper, finely diced

1 small red onion, finely diced

2 tomatoes, roughly chopped

1 clove garlic, minced

Leaves of ½ bunch fresh cilantro, roughly chopped

Juice of 1 lime

Juice of 1 lemon

Kosher salt and freshly ground pepper

Steak

1 Tbsp ancho chile powder

1 Tbsp smoked paprika

Kosher salt and freshly ground pepper

½ tsp garlic powder

6 oz (185 g) hanger steak

1 Tbsp olive oil

1 bag (8 oz/250 g) good-quality tortilla chips

1 can (15 oz/470 g) refried beans

4 oz (125 g) sharp Cheddar cheese, shredded (about 1 cup)

4 oz (125 g) cotija cheese, shredded (about 1 cup)

1 head romaine lettuce, finely shredded

2 Tbsp sour cream

1 bunch fresh chives, thinly sliced

STEAK NACHOS

SERVES 1 SUPER INCREDIBLY HUNGRY PERSON

When I get so hungry I can't think, sometimes I see a bag of chips and an old piece of Cheddar cheese and I know what I must do. Well, please do yourself a favor and plan ahead if only slightly, so that before you reach that point of no return, you've made a little salsa and seared some steak. You can thank me now but you'll thank yourself later. Eat this from the sheet tray while standing in your kitchen, cold beer in the other hand, because you are an animal and you had a hard day and you deserve it. — Max

Preheat the oven to 400°F (200°C).

To make the salsa, in a bowl, combine the peppers, onion, tomatoes, garlic, cilantro, and citrus juices. Season with salt and black pepper. Set aside at room temperature.

To make the steak, in a small bowl, stir together the chile powder, paprika, 1 teaspoon each salt and pepper, and the garlic powder. Dredge the steak in the spice mixture, coating it evenly.

In an ovenproof frying pan, warm the olive oil over high heat until it is smoking. Swirl the pan to coat the bottom evenly with the oil. Place the steak in the pan and sear, turning it once but otherwise not moving it, for 2 minutes on each side. Transfer to the oven and roast for 3 minutes. After 3 minutes, remove the pan from the oven and transfer the steak to a cutting board. Let rest for 10 minutes. Leave the oven on.

Spread the chips on a baking sheet and top with the refried beans and then both cheeses. Place in the oven and bake until the cheeses reach your desired level of meltedness, 5–10 minutes.

Remove the nachos from the oven and top with a layer of the lettuce. Carve the steak against the grain into thin slices. Place on top of the lettuce. Spoon the salsa evenly over the top. Dollop the sour cream on top of the salsa, garnish with the chives, and serve right away.

MEAT-LOAF BURGER

SERVES 1 HUNGRY PERSON

Yeah, Sherlock, you're seeing a trend here. Burgers are delicious, so yeah we decided to do two variations. And while a normal burger is a great thing to make for yourself, we didn't think the recipe was worth a whole page (for those of you interested, here it is: shape meat into ball. add salt. cook. eat). This meat-loaf burger is a whole 'nother story. It's a story that begins in a faraway land, where a man wanted all the fun of meat loaf without any of the bullshit. So he took his cow to the wise man of the village, paid him three silver coins, and behold! The recipe for the meat-loaf burger was forged. At least that's the story our parents used to tell us before bed.

6 oz (185 g) ground meat-loaf mix (beef, pork, and veal)

¼ cup (1 oz/30 g) panko bread crumbs

¼ cup (2 oz/60 g) grated yellow onion

1 large egg

2 Tbsp ketchup

1 clove garlic, minced

½ tsp soy sauce

¼ tsp red pepper flakes

Kosher salt

1 tsp olive oil

2 sesame buns, split and toasted

Good-quality mayonnaise for serving

2 large lettuce leaves or 1 cup (1½ oz/45 g) alfalfa sprouts

In a large bowl, combine the meat-loaf mix, bread crumbs, onion, egg, ketchup, garlic, soy sauce, red pepper flakes, and ¾ teaspoon salt and use your hands to mix; blend the ingredients well but work the meat as little as possible. (Overmixing can result in tough burgers.) Let rest at room temperature for 5 minutes.

In a nonstick frying pan, heat the olive oil over medium heat. While the oil is heating, using your hands, gently pat the burger mixture into 2 patties each about ¾ inch (2 cm) thick. When the oil is hot, place the patties in the pan and cook, turning once and taking care that the exterior of the burgers doesn't burn, for 2–3 minutes per side for medium-rare.

To serve, spread the cut sides of the buns with mayonnaise, tuck the burgers inside, and top with the lettuce. Serve right away, or wrap 1 burger in plastic, refrigerate, and eat it for lunch the next day.

1 cup (8 fl oz/250 ml) white balsamic vinegar

2 medium or 1 large artichoke

¼ cup (1½ oz/45 g) pitted Kalamata olives

1 Tbsp fresh lemon juice

¼ cup (4 fl oz/125 ml) extra-virgin olive oil, plus 2 Tbsp, or as needed

1 bunch rainbow chard

Kosher salt and freshly ground pepper

½ cup (3oz/90 g) golden raisins

Finely grated zest of 1 lemon

CHARD SALAD WITH ARTICHOKE HEARTS AND KALAMATA OLIVE VINAIGRETTE

SERVES 1–2

Artichokes are essentially two vegetables in one. In this recipe we use the heart, which is tender with a texture somewhere between a really creamy potato and a roasted turnip. But you can also eat the bottom part of the leaves; dip them into some homemade lemon aioli or melted butter with lemon juice mixed in. Serve the leaves as a snack while you're getting the rest of the meal ready. It's like the Tootsie Pop of vegetables. As Lil' Kim once said while singing about artichokes: How many leaves does it take to get to the center?

In a wide saucepan, combine 2 cups (16 fl oz/500 ml) water and the vinegar and bring to a boil over high heat.

While the water is heating, prepare the artichokes: Trim the stems to about 1 inch (2.5 cm). Using a large serrated knife, cut off the top one-third of each artichoke. Use a paring knife to nick off any remaining sharp tips from the outer leaves.

Add the artichokes to the boiling water. Reduce the heat to medium, cover, and cook until tender all the way through, 30–45 minutes. Insert the tip of the paring knife through a stem into the heart to check. Drain and let cool. Pull the leaves off each artichoke and snack on them or save for later. Discard the furry choke, using the tip of a teaspoon to scrape it out of the hearts, and trim off any tough parts. Cut the cleaned hearts into slices. Set aside.

In a blender or food processor, combine the olives and lemon juice and pulse to purée slightly. Add the ¼ cup (2 fl oz/60 ml) olive oil and process until smooth to make the vinaigrette. Set aside.

Cut the stems from the chard leaves. Cut the stems into narrow strips and coarsely chop the leaves, keeping the stems and leaves separate. In a large frying pan, heat the 2 tablespoons olive oil over medium-high heat. When the oil is hot, add the chard stems and a pinch of salt and cook, stirring occasionally, until softened, about 2 minutes. Using a slotted spoon, transfer to paper towels to drain, reserving the oil in the pan. Return the pan to medium heat (add more oil if the pan seems dry), add the chard leaves, and cook, stirring, just until wilted, about 2 minutes. Using tongs or the slotted spoon, transfer the leaves to a bowl, reserving the oil in the pan. Return the pan to medium-high heat (add more oil if the pan seems dry). When the oil is hot, add the artichoke pieces in a single layer and cook, turning once, until golden brown on both sides, about 2 minutes per side. Transfer to paper towels to drain briefly.

To assemble, add the chard stems and raisins to the chard leaves, pour in the vinaigrette (you may not need all of it), and toss to coat evenly. Transfer to a platter. Scatter the artichokes over the top, add a few grinds of pepper and the lemon zest, and serve warm with any remaining dressing on the side.

CHOPPED "CHEF'S" SALAD

SERVES 1 GENEROUSLY

You've definitely thought to yourself countless times "I should really just have a salad for dinner tonight." You may think you don't need a recipe for a chopped salad, but let's face it, you've never actually made one before. So here's the recipe. It's definitive. It's precise. It's tasty. It's supereasy. You probably have most of the ingredients already. And now you have no more excuses.

Kosher salt and freshly ground pepper

A small handful of green beans, trimmed

2 large eggs

About ¼ lb (125 g) arugula or mixed greens

2 plum tomatoes, cut into wedges, or 6 cherry tomatoes, halved

¼ cup (1½ oz/45 g) diced cooked turkey or ham

2 Tbsp diced salami

2 Tbsp crumbled blue, shredded Cheddar, or shredded Swiss cheese

1 small red onion, diced

2 Tbsp extra-virgin olive oil

1 Tbsp balsamic vinegar

Grated zest and juice of ½ lemon

1 tsp dried oregano

¼ tsp red pepper flakes

Bring a small stockpot three-fourths full of heavily salted water to a boil over high heat. Fill a large bowl with water and ice and set nearby.

Add the green beans to the boiling water and cook for 1 minute. Using a slotted spoon, transfer to the ice bath.

Let the water return to a boil, then add the eggs and set a timer for 8 minutes. Set up a second small ice bath. After 8 minutes, drain the eggs and place in the new ice bath.

In a large bowl, combine the arugula, tomatoes, turkey, salami, cheese, onion, and green beans and toss together gently. In a small bowl, whisk together the olive oil, vinegar, lemon zest and juice, oregano, red pepper flakes, and salt and black pepper to taste.

To assemble the salad, peel the eggs under cold running water and pat dry. Drizzle the dressing over the salad and toss gently to coat evenly. Transfer the salad to a large plate (or, since you're eating by yourself, just leave it in the bowl). Cut the eggs lengthwise into quarters, arrange on top of the salad, and eat right away.

Captain Dinner Party When the light faded and the darkness threatened to overwhelm all. When despair was sure to envelope hope, and evil was at the doorstep. When it looked like all was lost … a hero was born. A hero who promised a new era, one where potlucks didn't mean cold lentil loaf and only four cans of warm beer for 20 people. A hero who brought a new day of expertly planned and executed menus, of perfectly balanced cocktails. Born in a secret government lab experiment in which equal parts of DNA from Martha, James Kirk, Jay Gatbsy, and Denzel were mixed, Captain Dinner Party emerged. He threw parties for the government until he got sick of being a pawn in its games. Under the cover of night, he escaped to share his knowledge with us. Published for the first time, from leaked documents we've acquired, the secret knowledge on how to host a killer party is here for you. And so, Captain Dinner Party will always live on in all of us.

APOCALYPSE

100
**MIXED GREENS WITH ROASTED
STONE FRUIT AND GOAT BRIE**

103
THE RIB EYE

104
**SEARED SCALLOPS WITH
BULGUR AND PARSLEY OIL**

107
**PORK BELLY WITH
BACON-BLUEBERRY JAM AND MINT**

108
**GNOCCHI WITH ACORN SQUASH,
PANCETTA, AND CAMEMBERT**

COOK-IT-ALL-BEFORE
DINNER PARTY

112
**BRUSSELS SPROUTS WITH OIL-CURED
OLIVES, FETA, AND SOPRESSATA**

115
SPICY RATATOUILLE

116
ROSEMARY LAMB SHANKS

This is it. The last real meal you'll ever have. Sorry to be the bearer of bad news, but here comes the meteor–earthquake–alien invasion–thermonuclear war–dino-zombie attack. Spoiler alert: you're probably not going to make it. And maybe that's a good thing. Who wants to subsist on government rations and canned food? Who wants to forage to actually survive instead of foraging just being a cool way to feed rich people in Brooklyn? So tonight, go all out. Do all of the things that you've always thought of doing, like putting bacon on top of pork belly and shelling out the bucks for a ridiculously expensive dry-aged steak (the older, the better). Might as well make it count now, because soon those fifty-story-tall T. rex sharks will invade, earth will freeze over, and your neighbor is gonna try to eat your brains. And when that happens, in the words of our wise papa, you're going to be up shit creek without a paddle. So eat like there's no tomorrow, because in this case, it's the truth.

The camera zooms in close on your car. You are sweating profusely, cursing traffic, giving everyone the middle finger, cutting off a grandma who can barely see over the steering wheel. You are extremely late and monumentally frustrated. It's been a very bad day so far. And it's far from over.

NARRATOR "Your work meeting ran late. The line at the grocery store was 50 people long, and on top of that, your allergies are acting up! How will you make it home in time to cook dinner for your dinner-party guests?"

Your cursing reaches a fever pitch as you slam your hand down on the steering wheel over and over. Traffic will not budge.

NARRATOR "You haven't even made it out of the downtown rush-hour traffic, your guests are arriving in 10 minutes, and you still have to cook *everything*. Bad planning on your end! You are totally screwed. Might as well give up on life *right now*!"

You glance over at another car. The driver is singing her heart out to Taylor Swift. "How does she have it all together?" you think to yourself.

NARRATOR "Well, frustrated you—she used Max and Eli Sussman's Cook-It-All-Before Dinner party! (™). She's carefree and jamming out since she knows all of the food for her fantastic dinner party is ready to go! Have fun with your disappointed hungry guests. They'll never come over again!"

Cut to the sun-kissed backyard of the woman in the car next to you. She emerges from the kitchen onto her back deck looking stunning holding an icy-cold glistening beverage. Teeth twinkling. All of the food for her dinner party appears on the table just as the guests arrive. Everyone is wearing neutral-colored light sweaters, and she distributes white-wine spritzers. Everyone's hair is perfect. They all laugh at a joke in unison. Then, Tom Petty and the Heartbreakers appear and start playing a private show in her backyard. She's got a bounce house. And she's passing out stacks of $100 bills. Looks like a pretttyyyy amazing dinner party.

Cut back to you. Still stuck in traffic. Your cell phone dies. And then you run out of gas. Don't let this be you. Onward to the recipes.

FIRST WARM DAY

121
PAN-ROASTED TROUT WITH SUNFLOWER SEED–SUN-DRIED TOMATO PURÉE

122
LOBSTER SALAD WITH BIBB LETTUCE, APPLE, AND TARRAGON DRESSING

125
ASPARAGUS, BROCCOLI STEM, AND TOMATO SALAD

126
WARM YUKON POTATO SALAD

For those of you living in LA, here is a little primer. The rest of us deal with this thing called "seasons." There are four of them. One of them is called winter, and it's very cold. People get sad during this season and wear boots and 12 layers and stay inside and overpower the Netflix servers and complain about how they're freezing. There is another one called summer when it gets hot as shit and everyone starts to complain about how their AC is broken and how hard it is to sleep. But between those two extremes lies a magical moment called the first warm day of the year. It's like when the White Witch of Narnia lost her powers and everything melted and trees began to bud. People want to hang out all the time in the park on blankets, the sound of laughter fills the air, and folks break out into impromptu-choreographed dance routines *all the time*. This meal is for that day.

NIGHT AT THE CABIN

130
FRENCH ONION SOUP WITH GRUYÈRE

131
DUCK FAT POTATOES

133
GREEN BEAN AND EGG SALAD WITH DIJON-CAPER VINAIGRETTE

134
CASSOULENT

Have you ever noticed how French people are always impeccably dressed, drink wine at every meal, smoke cigarettes with reckless abandon, and still seem to live until they are 100? It's because they enjoy life more than the rest of us. They just have it all figured out. Daily fresh-baked baguettes and a one-month holiday do wonders for your stress level. So for a healthy state of mind, do as the French do. Take a holiday out to the countryside and rent a nice cabin with friends. Light the fireplace, let the wine breathe, and hide your cell phones and watches. There is nowhere you need to be. This is a dinner party for those who can fully let themselves be enveloped by a life of leisure. Channel your inner Serge Gainsbourg. Strum your guitar slowly, take three naps, read a book of poetry aloud. Dinner will be ready … when it's ready.

MIXED GREENS
WITH ROASTED STONE
FRUIT
AND GOAT BRIE

SERVES 4

This salad is deceptively simple. Charring the fruit and pairing it with tangy goat's milk Brie adds layers of complexity to this composition of just a few perfect ingredients. (You can use cow's milk Brie, but persevere in finding goat's milk, because it really elevates this dish to a standout.) Using flame is definitely the coolest way to brûlée the fruit, but in case you don't like the idea, we have included an oven alternative.

2–4 ripe peaches, apricots, plums, or other stone fruit, cut in half and pitted

1 tsp sugar

3 Tbsp white balsamic vinegar

2 Tbsp extra-virgin olive oil

½ tsp kosher salt

5 oz (155 g) mixed baby salad greens

3 oz (90 g) goat's milk or cow's milk Brie, at room temperature, broken into small bite-size pieces

Freshly ground pepper

In a bowl, toss the peaches with the sugar. Using tongs and working with ½ peach at a time, carefully heat the cut side of the peach over a gas flame until the sugar caramelizes and begins to char. It should be flecked with black parts but not burned. Alternatively, place the fruit, cut side up, on the countertop and char with a kitchen torch. (You can also place the fruit, cut side up, in a lightly oiled baking dish and roast in a 450°F/230°C oven until charred as described, about 10 minutes.) Let cool, then cut each half into 3 wedges.

In a small bowl, whisk together the vinegar, olive oil, and salt to make a vinaigrette.

In a bowl, combine the greens, Brie, and charred peaches, drizzle the vinaigrette over the top, and toss to coat evenly. Finish with a few cracks of pepper and serve right away.

One 1½–2½ lb (750 g–1.25 kg) bone-in rib eye steak, preferably prime and aged at least 30 days

Kosher salt and coarsely ground pepper

2 Tbsp extra-virgin olive oil

1 Tbsp unsalted butter

3 cloves garlic, smashed

3 fresh thyme sprigs

3 fresh rosemary sprigs

Coarse sea salt for garnish

THE RIB EYE

SERVES 4–6

Let the steak come to room temperature for 1–2 hours before cooking it.

About 10 minutes before you plan to start cooking the steak, season it well with kosher salt and pepper—start with about ½ cup (4 oz/125 g) salt and 2 tablespoons pepper. Coat the steak generously and evenly, then gently shake off the excess. Place on a wire rack and set aside at room temperature. Preheat the oven to 275°F (135°C).

In a frying pan large enough to accommodate the steak, warm the olive oil over medium-high heat. When the pan is smoking, add the steak and press down firmly to ensure even contact with the pan bottom. Let the steak cook, without moving it, for about 2 minutes. Carefully lift the steak, swirl the oil around in the pan, and flip the steak. Press down and cook on the second side for 2 minutes. Continue cooking the steak, flipping it in the same manner every 2 minutes, until the outer surface is deeply caramelized and dark brown, about 10 minutes total. At this point, flip the steak onto the rounded edge to render some of the fat.

Add the butter, garlic, and herb sprigs to the pan and, using a large spoon, baste over the steak with the fat and pan drippings. Flip and repeat. Reduce the heat to low until the butter has browned but not burned.

Transfer the steak to a clean wire rack set on top of a sheet tray. Pour the pan drippings into a heatproof bowl and reserve. Place the steak in the oven and bake, flipping every 3 minutes, until an instant-read thermometer inserted in the thickest part registers 125°F (52°C) for medium-rare.

Remove from the oven and let the meat rest without touching it (you don't want to disturb the juices) for at least 12 minutes. To carve, first cut off the bone: using a boning knife or a sharp paring knife, separate the meat from the bone as close to the bone as possible. You should see an arc-shaped piece on the opposite side of the meat from the bone; this is the deckle. Separate that from the eye by slicing between them. Cut the deckle into about 1-inch (2.5-cm) pieces. Remove any gristle or large pieces of fat. Cut the eye against the grain into slices ¼–½-inch (6–12 mm) thick.

To serve, divide the steak among individual plates. Drizzle with the pan drippings (rewarm if necessary), garnish with sea salt, and serve right away.

Dry aged just means hanging in a refrigerator for a while. The meat loses moisture, gains flavor, and ferments slightly, which adds some funkiness, too. The longer a steak is aged, the funkier and more tender it becomes. Usually the best you can get is a 28-day age, which is the minimum for any noticeable changes. This is a good starting point if it's your first time, but if you're adventurous, try scouting butcher shops for those that age even longer. Trust us, for the last night on earth, it's worth it. You can't take your money with you when you're gone, so you might as well get a 2½ pounder (1.25 kg).

SEARED SCALLOPS WITH BULGUR AND PARSLEY OIL

8 large dry sea scallops

1 cup (8 fl oz/250 ml) bottled clam juice or water

3 Tbsp extra-virgin olive oil, plus about 1 cup (8 fl oz/250 ml), well chilled

½ cup (3½ oz/105 g) medium-grain bulgur

½ cup (¾ oz/20 g) tightly packed fresh flat-leaf parsley leaves, roughly chopped

Kosher salt and freshly ground pepper

1 lemon, cut into wedges

SERVES 4

You should always buy your dry scallops the day that you plan to use them. We suggest going to an actual fish market in order to get the best-quality, freshest product available. You don't want scallops that have been injected with water or soaked in phosphate which is what grocery-store scallops have in order to extend their shelf life. Spend a little more, support your local fishmonger, and get a far superior product that will taste amazing and sear perfectly. — Max

Clean the scallops by first removing the foot from each—the small part at the edge of the body meat that is too tough to eat. The feet should peel off easily. If there is any visible sand or grit on the scallops, submerge them in cold water and swish around briefly and gently. Transfer to paper towels to drain.

In a saucepan, combine the clam juice and 1 tablespoon of the olive oil and bring to a boil over high heat. Reduce the heat to medium and add the bulgur. Cover tightly and simmer for 10 minutes. Remove from the heat and let stand, covered, for at least 10 minutes.

Make sure the cold olive oil is thoroughly chilled; this will help keep the parsley oil green. Put the parsley in a blender with a large pinch of salt. With the machine running, slowly stream in the 1 cup cold oil. When the parsley starts to break up and the mixture loosens, stop the blender and scrape down the sides of the jar. Start the blender again and slowly add more oil until the parsley is pulverized and the parsley oil is bright green and spoonable. Use only enough of the cold oil to make a smooth mixture.

Heat the remaining 2 tablespoons olive oil in a sauté pan over medium-high heat. (A nonstick pan is easier to work with, but a regular stainless-steel pan will give better caramelization.) Pat the scallops thoroughly dry with paper towels (drier than you think they need to be!). When the oil is smoking, season the scallops on all sides with salt and pepper. Carefully place them in the pan and cook, without moving them, for 1–2 minutes. The scallops should start showing a little golden color on the bottom edges. At this point, using a spatula or large spoon, peek underneath one. If the bottom of the scallop is a deep golden brown, flip it; if not, continue cooking for up to 1 minute more. After each scallop is turned, again cook without moving until deep golden brown on the second side, 1–2 minutes. Press the scallops lightly to test for doneness; they should yield. Do not cook them until hot all of the way through or they will be overcooked.

To serve, uncover the bulgur and fluff the grains with a fork. Spoon the bulgur onto a platter and arrange the scallops on top. Finish with a squeeze of lemon juice and a drizzle of the parsley oil (save the remaining oil for another use). Serve right away.

1 Tbsp sugar

2 tsp kosher salt

¼ lb (125 g) pork belly, skin removed

¼ lb (125 g) bacon, cut into ⅛-inch (3-mm) dice

¾ cup (7½ oz/235 g) blueberry jam

2 Tbsp extra-virgin olive oil

½ cup (2½ oz/75 g) peeled and sliced pear

8–10 fresh mint leaves, torn

PORK BELLY
WITH BACON-BLUEBERRY JAM
AND MINT

SERVES 4

In a small bowl, stir together the sugar and salt. Rub the mixture all over the pork belly. Cover and refrigerate for at least 4 hours or preferably overnight.

In a frying pan, cook the bacon over medium heat until crispy, about 5 minutes. Add the jam and stir to combine. Set aside and cover to keep warm.

Rinse off the pork belly and pat dry. Cut the pork belly into 4 equal slices each about 1 inch (2.5 cm) long by ½ inch (12 mm) thick. In a nonstick frying pan, heat the olive oil over medium-high heat. Add the pork belly and sear, turning once, until nicely caramelized on both sides, 2–3 minutes per side. Remove and dab on paper towels to drain.

Slice the pork belly at a long angle. To serve, place a few teaspoons of the bacon-blueberry jam on each plate. Top with slices of pork belly, alternating them with the pear slices. Garnish with the mint and serve right away.

When you buy the pork belly from your butcher, ask to have the skin removed. If you buy a packaged hunk of pork belly, the skin may still be on, but don't fear, as you'll be able to feel and see the harder top layer of skin that you should remove. Using a very sharp paring knife, make a small slit under the top layer of skin on the corner of the piece of belly. Slowly and confidently, cut under the skin while keeping as much of that tasty fat as you can.

GNOCCHI
WITH ACORN SQUASH
PANCETTA AND
CAMEMBERT

SERVES 4

The first time I had gnocchi I was a little kid at my nana and papa's best friend's house. They were rich and had a massive fancy house with this incredible glass collection, which made me feel like I was eating inside of a museum. So gnocchi has always felt like a decadent dish to me. I'll associate Dale Chihuly with soft, fluffy potato pillows forever. — Eli

1 acorn squash (about 2 lb/1 kg)

1 Tbsp extra-virgin olive oil, plus 1 tsp

Kosher salt

4 oz (125 g) pancetta, cut into ½-inch (12-mm) dice (about 1 cup)

1 yellow onion, cut into 1-inch (2.5-cm) cubes

1 clove garlic, crushed

6 oz (185 g) cremini mushrooms, stemmed, brushed clean, and halved (or quartered if very large)

¼ cup (2 fl oz/60 ml) dry white wine

1 tsp chopped fresh thyme, plus sprigs for garnish

½ tsp chopped fresh sage

1 lb (500 g) potato gnocchi

2 oz (60 g) Camembert cheese, broken up into 1-inch (2.5-cm) chunks, at room temperature

1 tsp sherry vinegar

Preheat the oven to 350°F (180°C). Line a sheet tray with parchment paper.

Cut the squash in half. Scrape out the seeds and stringy membranes with a spoon. Brush the cut sides with the 1 tablespoon olive oil and sprinkle with 1 teaspoon salt. Place the halves, cut side down, on the prepared pan and sprinkle with ¼ cup (2 fl oz/60 ml) water. Bake until tender, about 45 minutes. Remove from the oven and let the squash cool completely. Remove the skin and discard. Break up the flesh into large bite-size chunks. Set aside.

Bring a pot three-fourths full of generously salted water to a boil.

While the water is heating, in a large frying pan, heat the 1 teaspoon olive oil over medium heat. Add the pancetta and cook, stirring to brown on all sides and to prevent sticking, until some of the fat has rendered, about 5 minutes. Add the onion and garlic and cook until the aromatics are slightly softened and beginning to caramelize, about 5 minutes longer. Add the mushrooms and cook, stirring often, until the mushrooms are softened and the pancetta is crispy, 3–5 minutes longer. Adjust the heat as necessary to ensure that the pancetta is cooking but not burning.

Pour in the wine and stir to scrape up any browned bits on the bottom of the pan. Stir in the chopped thyme and sage. Remove from the heat, cover to keep warm, and set aside.

Add the gnocchi to the boiling water and cook until al dente, according to the package directions.

Drain the gnocchi, reserving some of the cooking water, and add to the pan with the pancetta mixture. Add the squash, Camembert, and vinegar and toss just until everything is combined and warmed through. Add some of the reserved pasta water if the mixture seems dry. Serve right away, garnished with the thyme sprigs.

HOW TO THROW THE BEST PARTY EVER

THAT EVERYONE WILL STILL—MAYBE, HOPEFULLY—REMEMBER TOMORROW

MAX Most of the stuff you read about how to entertain is pretty much pointless, out of touch, and a big waste of your money and time. No one is going to go home and talk about how great the centerpiece was. They are only going to remember if they had fun or not. And the key ingredients to having fun are painfully obvious: great food, great music, and plenty to drink.

ELI The secret to having a sweet soiree isn't alliteration icebreakers, board games, goodie bags, floral arrangements, or tablecloths. Those things are the secret to getting made fun of at your own party. So unless you're having a this-is-my-seventh-grade birthday-themed party or you're channeling Ina, don't overwork yourself. The real way to throw an epic slam bash or even just a dope casual dinner party is to be prepared with the food and to delegate the remaining responsibility to your guests.

MAX The last thing you want to be doing during your own party is running out to get something that someone else could have brought on their way over.

ELI Ice runs are the bane of my existence.

MAX Or running out to get more cups. Or really going out for anything at all. Who the hell wants to leave their own party? (Well, sometimes I actually do). But what

people don't do well enough before parties is to make people commit to bringing certain things.

ELI Since we always supply the bulk of the food, I make a list of the guests and then write next to their name what I am delegating them to bring.

MAX That's very fascist.

ELI My party is not a democratic party, Max, which is why even though we live together, I'm referring to it as my party. If it saves me money and also the headache of last-minute hassles, I'll play the rigid party thrower in this scenario. So, yeah, I told you to bring a salad (the Brussels sprouts with olives, feta, and sopressata on page 112 will do) and I really want you to bring it (like Torrance Shipman does in the classic tale of triumphing over adversity, *Bring It On*). I don't think it is too much to ask you to bring something in exchange for you turning my beautiful apartment into your own Champagne bubble bath.

MAX Yeah, it might be your last night on earth (see Apocalypse, page 96) and you are opening up your home to people who might be your only partners in this new post-apocalyptic society. If you can't trust someone to bring the pretzel bites (page 55),

how can you trust them to barter away their offspring for gasoline or antibiotics?

ELI Batch out a cocktail (pages 46–47), so that once the party starts to fill up, you're ready to go. And it's not the worst thing to not be 100 percent ready with food prep. Everyone is going to ask if they can help out so there might as well be some work left for them to do making the *jamón y queso* bites (page 52).

MAX Start out with a little snack time, and put the food and booze in different locations to help open the room up. If you can't get it together to make a playlist, force a friend to build it. Otherwise, you will fall into a dark web-radio spiral, or someone will just put on the new Beyoncé over and over and over. I've been there, and it doesn't end well.

ELI I love Beyoncé almost as much as I love Destiny's Child. And my last suggestion: no goodie bags.

MAX You only need to give out a goodie bag if it's actually the Apocalypse. Then it'd be a pretty classy move to send everyone off into the world with at least a first-aid kit and a flashlight. It's only a matter of time until AA batteries are worth more than gold, and people will only be as valuable to the collective as their survival skills make them, like the ability to suture a wound and build a shelter. I for one have been stockpiling copper wire and antibiotics behind a false wall in my bedroom for years. So, basically, I'm ready.

ELI OK, pump the brakes, captain crazy . . . thank god one of us is stockpiling. Well, even if said Apocalypse (that I am clearly ill-prepared for) doesn't happen, after the party we threw, the revelers might still feel like it is, so throwing them a ziploc bag with a few aspirins in it as they leave really says, "Hope you enjoyed the party."

BRUSSELS SPROUTS WITH OIL-CURED OLIVES FETA AND SOPRESSATA

SERVES 4

In the late 1980s and early 1990s, a man with a raw mix of graceful power, a funny accent, and a sweet fake name emerged on the scene, forever changing the face of action films. The Muscles from Brussels, a.k.a. Jean-Claude Van Damme, took up karate as a boy and ballet as a teen. His best film is probably *Bloodsport*, though *Timecop* and *Hard Target* have some sweet parts, too. While the Oscar still eludes him, we're holding out hope that his next film, *Revenge Face Punch 2*, will bring home the gold.

6 Tbsp (3 fl oz/90 ml) extra-virgin olive oil

¼ cup (2 fl oz/60 ml) fresh lemon juice

Kosher salt

1 lb (500 g) Brussels sprouts, sliced very thinly on a mandoline or with a sharp chef's knife

1 cup (5 oz/155 g) pitted oil-cured black olives

2 oz (60 g) sopressata or other spicy dry salami, cut into ⅛-inch (3-mm) dice

1 tsp chopped fresh marjoram or oregano

2 oz (60 g) feta cheese, crumbled

In a large bowl, whisk together the olive oil, lemon juice, and ½ teaspoon salt.

Add the Brussels sprouts, olives, sopressata, and marjoram to the bowl and stir to mix well and coat the sprouts with the vinaigrette. Cover and refrigerate for at least 30 minutes or up to 4 hours.

Before serving, bring to room temperature. Fold in the feta, then taste and adjust the seasoning.

SPICY RATATOUILLE

1 globe eggplant, trimmed and cut into 1-inch (2.5-cm) cubes

3 zucchini, trimmed and cut into 1-inch (2.5-cm) cubes

1 large yellow onion, cut into 1-inch (2.5-cm) cubes

¼ cup (2 fl oz/60 ml) extra-virgin olive oil, plus 2 Tbsp

Kosher salt

1 can (28 oz/875 g) whole tomatoes, with juice

2 cloves garlic, minced

¼ cup (2 fl oz/60 ml) sherry vinegar or red wine vinegar

1 tsp sugar

¾ tsp red pepper flakes, or more to taste

2 small sprigs *each* fresh marjoram, thyme, and rosemary

Gremolata Bread Crumbs

2 Tbsp extra-virgin olive oil

1 small clove garlic, minced

1 cup (4 oz/125 g) panko bread crumbs

2 Tbsp minced fresh flat-leaf parsley

Kosher salt

Grated zest of 1 lemon

SERVES 4

Only Pixar could make a rat seem like a cute, cool friend that you'd want to hang out with. And only we could take a traditional French Provençal dish of stewed vegetables and improve on an already incredible classic. We top our version with *gremolata* bread crumbs, which we are confident would make Julia Child shriek with glee.

Preheat the oven to 475°F (245°C).

Pile the eggplant, zucchini, and onion on a large sheet tray. Drizzle with the ¼ cup (2 fl oz/60 ml) olive oil and sprinkle with 1 teaspoon salt. Toss to mix and coat well with the oil. Spread in an even layer and roast until soft and caramelized, 30–45 minutes. Stir halfway through to ensure even cooking. Remove from the oven and set aside.

Chop the tomatoes roughly, or process them to a coarse purée in a blender or food processor. Set aside.

In a large saucepan, heat the 2 tablespoons olive oil over medium heat. Add the garlic and sauté for 1 minute. Add the tomatoes and vinegar, bring to a simmer, and cook for 10 minutes, stirring often. Add the roasted vegetables, sugar, red pepper flakes, and herb sprigs and simmer until the flavors have blended and the juices have thickened, 15–20 minutes.

Meanwhile, make the bread crumbs: In a frying pan, heat the olive oil over medium heat. Add the garlic and sauté for 1 minute. Add the bread crumbs and toast, stirring constantly, until golden brown, about 3 minutes. Remove from the heat and stir in the parsley, ¼ teaspoon salt, and the lemon zest. Remove from the heat and let cool completely. (The seasoned bread crumbs will keep in an airtight container at room temperature for up to 1 week.)

To serve, sprinkle the ratatouille with the bread crumbs.

ROSEMARY
LAMB SHANKS

SERVES 4

One of the best things about these shanks is that you're going to end up with a good amount of delicious lamb fat as you skim this dish. *Do not* throw away that lamb fat. We get it, you're one of those healthy, juice-loving, exercising weirdos and you're saying "What am I going to do with lamb fat?" And we're here to tell you. Spread it on toast and bake in a 400°F (200°C) oven. Mix it into beans or fry potatoes in it. Put it in your coffee. Lamb fat is delicious. It will be good in *everything*.

2 Tbsp vegetable oil

4 lamb shanks, each about ¾ lb (375 g) and 6 inches (15 cm) long

Kosher salt

1 yellow onion, cut into 1-inch (2.5-cm) cubes

4 heads garlic, cloves peeled and lightly crushed

1 cup (8 fl oz/250 ml) dry white wine

1 cup (8 fl oz/250 ml) chicken stock

1 can (28 oz/875 g) whole tomatoes, with juice

1 tsp brown sugar

1 tsp red pepper flakes, or more to taste

4 large fresh thyme sprigs

2 large fresh rosemary sprigs

Steamed white or brown rice, for serving

In a large Dutch oven or other wide, heavy-bottomed pot with tall sides, heat the vegetable oil over medium-high heat. While the oil is heating, lightly season the lamb shanks with salt. Add the shanks to the pot and sear until nicely browned on all sides, turning as needed to ensure even color, 10–15 minutes total. Work in batches, if necessary, to avoid crowding the pot.

Using tongs, transfer the shanks to a plate and set aside. Reduce the heat to medium and add the onion to the fat in the pot. Sauté until soft, about 5 minutes. Add the garlic and sauté until the garlic is soft and the onion is lightly browned, about 5 minutes longer.

Add the wine and bring to a simmer. Let reduce slightly, about 10 minutes. Use a wooden spoon or a spatula to scrape up any browned bits from the bottom of the pot and stir to dissolve them in the liquid. Add the chicken stock, tomatoes, brown sugar, red pepper flakes, and herb sprigs and stir. Return to a simmer, break up the tomatoes with the spoon, and place the lamb shanks in the pot. Adjust the heat as needed to maintain a gentle simmer. Cook, uncovered, until the meat starts to fall off the bone, 2–3 hours.

Remove from the heat and let cool slightly. Skim off as much fat as possible from the surface (reserve for another use, such as in place of olive oil when roasting potatoes or cooking rice). To serve, place some rice on each plate and arrange a lamb shank on top. Spoon some of the juices in the pot over everything.

4 firm beefsteak tomatoes, quartered and cored

8 Fresno peppers

4 cloves garlic

4 fresh thyme sprigs

6 Tbsp (3 fl oz/90 ml) extra-virgin olive oil, or more if needed

Kosher salt and freshly ground pepper

1 cup (4 oz/125 g) sunflower seeds, toasted

1 cup (8 oz/250 g) chopped drained oil-packed sun-dried tomatoes

4 skin-on trout fillets, about 6 oz (185 g) each

1 bunch dandelion greens (about 10 oz/315 g) or chicory

1 lemon, halved

PAN-ROASTED TROUT WITH SUNFLOWER SEED SUN-DRIED TOMATO PURÉE

SERVES 4

The sauce in this recipe is bright and fresh and makes us think of romesco. (Missed our version? See page 113 in *This is a Cookbook*.) We wanted to give you another sauce in this cookbook that's a perfect dipping, spreading, and use-it-all-any-which-way sauce. There is going to be extra left over and we like to snack on it with toasted hunks of sourdough bread, or poured over rice, steamed vegetables, or even as a sauce for chicken. It should be clear to you that we are obsessed with putting this sauce on *everything*.

Preheat the oven to 400°F (200°C). Line a large sheet tray with parchment paper. Pile the fresh tomatoes, peppers, garlic, and thyme on the prepared pan, drizzle with 2 tablespoons of the oil, season generously with salt, and toss to coat evenly. Spread in an even layer and roast until the peppers and tomatoes begin to soften and the skins begin to char, 25–30 minutes. Remove from the oven, let cool, and discard the thyme.

Transfer half of the roasted vegetables to a blender. With the machine on medium speed, add half each of the sunflower seeds and sun-dried tomatoes. Raise the speed to high and blend for 1 minute. If the mixture is not moving freely, slowly add more oil and water, in alternating teaspoons, until it flows. Pour the sauce into a large bowl. Repeat with the remaining vegetables, sunflower seeds, and tomatoes, and mix with the first batch. Taste and adjust the seasoning. Set aside.

Place the trout, skin side up, on a plate, top with a double layer of paper towels, and let stand for about 5 minutes to absorb the excess moisture. Meanwhile, heat 2 tablespoons of the oil in a large sauté pan over medium heat. Add the dandelion greens and toss until wilted and darker green, about 2 minutes. Season with salt and pepper and cook until tender, about 1 minute longer. Transfer to a paper towel–lined plate to drain. Squeeze ½ lemon over the top.

Wipe the pan clean, add the remaining 2 tablespoons oil, and place over medium-high heat. Discard the paper towels from the trout and sprinkle the skin side generously with salt. Place the fish, skin side down, in the hot oil and cook the fillets, without moving them, until the flesh is cooked three-fourths of the way through (the flesh will turn opaque). Using a wide spatula, carefully flip the fillets and cook for just 10 seconds longer. Immediately transfer the fillets, skin side up, to a cutting board.

To serve, arrange the greens on a serving platter. Top with the fillets, skin side up, and squeeze the remaining ½ lemon over the fillets. Serve right away. Pass the sauce at the table (any leftover sauce will keep for up to 2 weeks).

LOBSTER SALAD
WITH BIBB LETTUCE
APPLE
AND TARRAGON DRESSING

1 Granny Smith apple

Juice of 1 lemon

2 large shallots, thinly sliced

2 Tbsp extra-virgin olive oil

2 Tbsp cider vinegar

Kosher salt and freshly ground pepper

½ lb (250 g) fresh-cooked lobster meat, torn into bite-size pieces; lump crabmeat, picked over for cartilage and shell fragments; or peeled shrimp

½ cup (4 oz/125 g) plain yogurt

2 Tbsp fresh tarragon leaves, finely chopped

1 head butter (Bibb) lettuce, cored and separated into leaves

SERVES 4

There's something perfectly calming about the new-wave 1980s band The B52s' song "Rock Lobster." It's got this chill beachy vibe that's just oozing 1960s California cool. This salad is a throwback itself. It's definitely a ladies-that-lunch type of salad, and we want to bring it mainstream and to the masses. We know that people are going to be digging around looking for lobster hunks, so chop the pieces real small so that the lobster is well distributed and fair for everyone. You don't want your guests feeling like you went to Zabar's.

Core and quarter the apple, then cut the quarters lengthwise into slices about ⅛ inch (3 mm) thick. Put in a small bowl, toss with the lemon juice, and set aside.

In another small bowl, toss the shallots with the olive oil, vinegar, and ½ teaspoon salt and let stand at room temperature for 10 minutes.

In a large bowl, toss the lobster meat with the yogurt. Add the apple and shallots, along with any liquid left in the bowls, and the tarragon and toss gently to mix. Taste and adjust the seasoning. Add the lettuce and toss to mix.

To serve, arrange the salad on individual plates, dividing it evenly. Finish with a few grinds of black pepper. Serve right away.

ASPARAGUS
BROCCOLI STEM
AND TOMATO SALAD

Vinaigrette

2 Tbsp extra-virgin olive oil

2 Tbsp sherry vinegar

1 Tbsp Mae Ploy sweet chili sauce

1 Tbsp honey

Kosher salt

1 bunch medium-thick asparagus, tough, woody ends snapped off

1 head broccoli

1⅓ cups (8 oz/250 g) cherry, grape, or pear tomatoes, preferably a mix of colors, halved or thinly sliced

¼ cup (1½ oz/45 g) pine nuts, toasted

SERVES 4

In this recipe, the asparagus is blanched and the broccoli is raw. It's a perfect warm-day salad because it's crispy and fresh tasting with just a little bit of heat from the chile sauce. You are going to be left with a lot of broccoli florets, which means that you should make the Crispy Rice with Broccoli and Teriyaki Sauce (page 36).

To make the vinaigrette, in a small bowl or glass measuring cup, whisk together the olive oil, vinegar, chili sauce, and honey until emulsified. Set aside at room temperature to allow the flavors to blend while you make the salad.

Fill a large pot three-fourths full of water and stir in enough salt to make it taste quite salty, like the ocean. Bring to a boil over high heat. Fill a large bowl with water and ice and set nearby.

Cut the asparagus on the bias ⅛ inch (3 mm) thick. Set aside.

Separate the broccoli stem from the florets where it starts to branch out. (Reserve the florets for another use.) Peel off the darker green fibrous part of the stem using a vegetable peeler. If there are any nooks and crannies of peel, use a paring knife to remove them. Cut the stem in half lengthwise, then cut into matchsticks the same shape as the asparagus. Put in a large bowl and set aside.

When the water is boiling, carefully slide in all of the asparagus at once. Cook for 1 minute, then drain in a colander set in the sink. Immediately submerge in the ice water for at least 10 minutes, then drain and pat dry completely.

To assemble, add the asparagus and tomatoes to the bowl with the broccoli stems. Pour in the vinaigrette and toss to mix and coat well. Place on a platter, garnish with the pine nuts, and serve right away.

WARM YUKON POTATO SALAD

SERVES 4–6

We don't get down with mayo-based potato salads. They get soggy, gloppy, and heavy, and it feels like you just ate a cup of mayonnaise (which you probably did). This potato salad is more like you just opened up a bottle of springtime and poured the whole thing over some boiled potatoes. It's light and refreshing. It's basically the Prosecco of potato salad.

1 lb (500 g) Yukon gold potatoes
Kosher salt

Vinaigrette
¼ cup (2 fl oz/60 ml) extra-virgin olive oil
⅓ cup (3 fl oz/80 ml) cider vinegar
1 tsp Dijon mustard
1 tsp sugar
Kosher salt

½ cup (¾ oz/20 g) packed fresh flat-leaf parsley leaves, finely chopped
1 bunch green onions, white and tender green parts only, trimmed and cut into slices ¼ inch (6 mm) thick

Put the potatoes in a saucepan and add cold water to cover. Bring to a boil over high heat, then stir in 1 teaspoon salt. Reduce the heat to medium and cook until tender throughout, 20–30 minutes. (The timing depends on the size and age of the potatoes; slide a thin-bladed knife through a potato to test. It should slide smoothly all the way through without resistance.)

Meanwhile, make the vinaigrette: In a small bowl or glass measuring cup, whisk together the olive oil, vinegar, mustard, sugar, 1 teaspoon salt, and 2 tablespoons water until emulsified and smooth. Taste and adjust the seasoning. Set aside.

When the potatoes are done, drain in a colander set in the sink and let cool slightly. Pat dry and put in a large bowl. Using your hands if you are super tough or a large spoon if you are not, smash the potatoes into smaller pieces.

Whisk half of the parsley and half of the green onions into the vinaigrette. Pour into the bowl with the potatoes and toss to mix and coat well. Taste and adjust the seasoning. Garnish with the remaining parsley and green onions. Serve while still warm. (The potato salad will keep, tightly covered in the fridge, for up to 3 days.)

FRENCH ONION SOUP WITH GRUYÈRE

SERVES 4

Besides chicken soup, is there anything more comforting than a rich beef stock topped with a crispy, bubbly sheet of delicious melty cheese? It's the food equivalent of a teddy bear wearing a snuggie and holding a cup of hot cocoa asking you to cuddle.

3 Tbsp unsalted butter

¼ cup (2 fl oz/60 ml) dry white wine

2 large yellow onions, cut into julienne

Kosher salt

4 cups (1 l) good-quality low-sodium beef stock

1 fresh thyme sprig

½ French baguette, cut on the diagonal into slices ½ inch (12 mm) thick, to make 4 big croutons about 4 inches (10 cm) long

8 oz (250 g) Gruyère cheese, shredded (about 2 cups)

In a large sauté pan over medium heat, gently melt 2 tablespoons of the butter in the wine. Add the onions and sprinkle 1 teaspoon salt evenly over the top. Cook, stirring often, until the onions begin to soften, about 10 minutes. Reduce the heat to low and cook, still stirring often, until the onions are deeply caramelized and dark golden brown, about 1 hour.

Pour the beef stock over the caramelized onions and stir to scrape up any browned bits on the bottom of the pan. Add the thyme, cover to keep warm, and set aside.

Preheat the oven to 425°F (220°C).

In an ovenproof frying pan, melt the remaining 1 tablespoon butter over medium heat. Place the baguette slices in the pan and toast until they are golden brown on the underside, about 3 minutes. Flip over so the toasted side is exposed and cover the toasted side of each slice with the cheese, dividing it evenly. Toast in the oven until the cheese is bubbly, about 5 minutes.

Discard the thyme sprig from the soup. Ladle the soup into individual bowls, dividing the onions evenly. Cover each portion with a cheesy crouton and serve right away.

DUCK FAT POTATOES

1 cup (8 fl oz/250 ml) cider vinegar

1 serrano or 2 jalapeño peppers, cut into slices ¼ inch (6 mm) thick

Kosher salt

3 lb (1.5 kg) russet potatoes

4 cups (1 l) vegetable oil

2 cups (1 lb/500 g) rendered duck fat

SERVES 4–6

In a bowl, stir together the vinegar, pepper, and 1 teaspoon salt and set aside.

Put the potatoes in a saucepan and add cold water to cover. Bring to a boil over high heat, then stir in 2 tablespoons salt. Reduce the heat to medium and cook until the potatoes are tender but not falling apart when pierced, about 20 minutes.

Meanwhile, in a deep fryer or a saucepan with tall sides, combine the oil and duck fat and heat to 350°F (180°C), stirring the duck fat after it melts to mix well.

When the potatoes are done, drain and then let cool until you can handle them. Use a fork to split the potatoes into 2–3-inch (5–7.5-cm) pieces.

Working in batches if needed to avoid crowding the pot, carefully place the potatoes in the hot fat and fry until golden brown and crispy, about 10 minutes. Using a skimmer or slotted spoon, transfer the potatoes to paper towels to drain and season lightly with salt while still warm.

Arrange on a serving platter and drizzle the vinegar sauce over the top. Serve right away, passing additional sauce at the table (leftover sauce can be stored in an airtight container in the refrigerator for up to 2 weeks).

This is one of those WTF-not? moments in the cookbook. Sure, you can use regular ol' oil to cook these potatoes, but why would you possibly want to do that when we've presented you with the opportunity and know-how to make *duck fat* potatoes. It's like if we provided you with the choice to continue driving your Honda with the CD player … or let's take a few minutes to teach you how to drive stick and you can take the Lamborghini for a spin with Prince in the passenger seat singing live.

3 Tbsp extra-virgin olive oil

¾ lb (375 g) green beans or mix of
green beans and yellow wax beans,
ends trimmed

3 Tbsp Dijon mustard

2 Tbsp brine-packed capers,
drained and patted dry

Kosher salt and freshly ground
pepper

4 large eggs, hard boiled, peeled,
and halved lengthwise

GREEN BEAN
AND EGG SALAD
WITH DIJON-CAPER VINAIGRETTE

SERVES 4

In a large frying pan, heat the olive oil over medium-high heat. When the oil is hot, add the beans and toss to coat well with the oil. Then let the beans cook, without moving them, for 2 minutes. Stir well and let cook undisturbed for 2–3 minutes longer. You want much of the outsides of the beans to be blistered and blackened but not burned. Remove the pan from the heat.

Add the mustard and capers to the pan and stir to mix well with the beans and the oil. Add a splash of water if the beans seem too dry. Season with salt and pepper.

Transfer to a platter, tuck the eggs in among the beans, and serve right away.

We love us some haricots. GB's are tasty blanched, fried, in salads, or as the main star of the dish. This dish is incredibly simple and should be made last, right before serving. So make sure the potatoes are crispy, the cassoulent is steaming, and the cheese on the onion soup is starting to melt and bubble and then, only then, should you make this for the table. — **Max**

CASSOULENT

SERVES 4–6

Cholent is an Eastern European–style of Jew-stew that we grew up eating, especially on winter Saturdays when our parents took us to a Jewish house of worship called a synagogue. (Did you know you'd learn so much about Judaism from this pork-filled cookbook?) This recipe takes elements from both *cholent* and the French cassoulet to make something brand-new. It's an evolved rustic stew for the progressive eater. What could be better than the stew brainchild of the flavor-obsessed French and the "are you full yet?" obsessed Jews?

3 cups (24 fl oz/750 ml) chicken stock, heated almost to a boil

½ cup (3½ oz/105 g) pearl barley

2 pieces duck confit

¾ lb (375 g) cooked corned beef, cut into 1-inch (2.5-cm) pieces

½ lb (250 g) smoked beef or pork sausages

1 can (15½ oz/485 g) cannellini beans, drained but not rinsed

1 lb (500 g) russet potatoes, peeled and cut into ¾-inch (2-cm) cubes

½ cup (2 oz/60 g) cippolini onions

½ lb (250 g) carrots, peeled and cut crosswise into 1-inch (2.5-cm) pieces

3 cloves garlic, coarsely chopped

½ tsp cayenne pepper

Kosher salt and freshly ground pepper

1 tsp cornstarch

In a small saucepan, bring 1½ cups (12 fl oz/375 ml) of the chicken stock to a boil over high heat. Stir in the barley, reduce the heat to maintain a gentle simmer, cover, and cook until tender and the stock is absorbed, about 45 minutes.

Preheat the oven to 350°F (180°C).

Pick the meat and skin off the bones of the duck confit pieces and put them in a large Dutch oven or other wide, heavy-bottomed pot with tall sides. Discard the bones. Add the corned beef, sausages, cannellini beans, potatoes, onions, carrots, garlic, cayenne, 1 teaspoon salt, and ½ teaspoon pepper to the pot. In a medium bowl, make a slurry by adding the cornstarch to 2 tablespoons of the stock and mixing to dissolve. Stir or whisk in the remaining stock and then pour the cornstarch mixture into the pot and stir to mix well.

When the barley is cooked, add it to the pot and stir to distribute evenly.

Cover the pot, put it in the oven, and braise for 40 minutes. Uncover and braise until the liquid is absorbed and the potatoes are tender, 20–30 minutes longer. To test for doneness, bite into a potato cube; if it's not tender all the way through, cook for a few more minutes until done. If the stew seems a little dry, add a little stock or water.

To serve, spoon the stew onto plates or into pasta plates or bowls. Serve right away.

NO REGRETS

No Regrets When you reflect back on your life, what kind of person will you see? Someone who was cautious at every turn? Someone who made lists of pros and cons before any decision? Someone who counted calories and never had any fun? Someone who asked rhetorical questions about others' decisions? Or will you see someone who lived life to the fullest by skydiving naked, jumping on the field at the Super Bowl, running with the bulls in Pamplona, fighting Laila Ali, yelling "I hate the Yankees" in Yankee stadium, driving a motorcycle up a ramp and across a fiery moat, climbing Mt. Everest, and eating dessert with no regrets? The choice is yours.

PARMESAN CAKE WITH BLACKBERRY JAM AND WHIPPED CREAM

MAKES ONE 9-BY-12-INCH (23-BY-30-CM) CAKE; SERVES 6–8

After the first time making this, it didn't look as I'd envisioned. I was bummed. My head hanging low, I offered a taste to a friend who, to my great surprise, said "This is amazing!" And in my head I heard this soaring voice-over by Morgan Freeman: "And the people of the land liked the Parmesan shortcake like they had never liked a dessert before. And then, little by little, things began to change for the better. And one day... many years later, their children's children sat with their children... telling tales about the way life used to be. Back in the time... of Parmesan cake." — Eli

1 cup (5 oz/155 g) all-purpose flour

½ cup (4 oz/125 g) sugar, plus 2 Tbsp

¼ cup (1½ oz/45 g) baking powder

4 hard-boiled egg yolks

¼ tsp kosher salt

½ cup (4 oz/125 g) cold unsalted butter, cut into small cubes

2 cups (16 fl oz/500 ml) heavy cream

4 oz (125 g) Parmesan cheese, grated (about 1 cup)

2 cups (1¼ lb/625 g) blackberry or boysenberry jam

Preheat the oven to 350°F (180°C). Have ready a 9-by-12-inch (23-by-30-cm) baking dish.

In a food processor, combine the flour, the ½ cup sugar, the baking powder, egg yolks, and salt and process until well combined. Add the butter cubes and pulse just until the mixture is the consistency of a coarse meal. With the machine running, add the ½ cup (4 fl oz/125 ml) cream in a slow, steady stream and process until the dough comes together. Stop the machine, sprinkle in the cheese, and pulse until incorporated.

Use a rubber spatula to transfer the batter to the baking dish and spread in an even layer. Bake for 10 minutes, then rotate the dish 180 degrees. Bake until the top is golden brown, about 15 minutes longer.

Remove the cake from the oven and let cool in the baking dish on a wire rack for about 15 minutes. Meanwhile, in a bowl, whisk together the remaining ½ cup (4 fl oz/125 ml) cream and the 2 tablespoons sugar until soft peaks form.

To serve, cut the warm cake into squares with a knife or into rounds with a cookie cutter and transfer to individual plates or shallow bowls. Or crumble the cake into pieces onto the plates or into the bowls. Spoon some of the whipped cream onto each serving and top with the jam.

One 2-lb (1 kg) loaf challah, homemade (page 150) or purchased, torn into 2-inch (5-cm) pieces

½ cup (4 oz/125 g) unsalted butter, cut into small cubes, plus 2 Tbsp, melted

½ cup (4 fl oz/125 ml) whole milk

5 large eggs, beaten

2 tsp pure vanilla extract

1 tsp almond extract

½ cup (4 oz/125 g) sugar, plus 3 Tbsp

1 Tbsp ground cinnamon

1 tsp kosher salt

1 pint (8 oz/250) strawberries, stemmed and quartered

2 Tbsp fresh lemon juice

2 cups (16 fl oz/500 ml) heavy cream

VANILLA-ALMOND
BAKED
CHALLAH

SERVES 8

This recipe falls somewhere on the dessert spectrum between French toast and bread pudding. Where does it fall on the tasty taste spectrum? Somewhere just to the left of "will make your face melt like you're two feet away from a Robert Plant solo" and to the right of "will make your heart race like you're strapped to the chest of a full-grown lion and you're skydiving."

Preheat the oven to 400°F (200°C).

In large bowl, combine the challah, butter cubes, milk, eggs, vanilla, almond extract, the ½ cup (4 oz/125 g) sugar, the cinnamon, and the salt. Toss well with your hands to distribute and incorporate all of the ingredients evenly. It's okay if the butter cubes stay somewhat intact.

Grease a 9-by-12-inch (23-by-30-cm) or 8-inch (20-cm) square baking dish with the melted butter. Pile the bread mixture loosely in the pan, spread evenly, and then press down to reform a rough loaf. It doesn't need to be tightly packed. If the butter cubes don't look evenly distributed, do your best to redistribute them. Also, you don't want an area where there is no bread, or when the butter melts, you will be left with an open space. Bake until a golden brown crust forms on top, 20–30 minutes.

Meanwhile, in a bowl, combine the strawberries, the 3 tablespoons sugar, and the lemon juice. Toss to mix well and set aside. In another bowl, whisk the cream until stiff peaks form.

When the challah is done, transfer to a wire rack and let cool for about 10 minutes. Cut into squares and transfer to individual plates. Top each serving with a dollop of the whipped cream and some strawberries.

PISTACHIO HALVA

2 cups (1 lb/500 g) tahini

1½ cups (12 oz/375 g) sugar

Kosher salt

½ tsp almond extract

1 cup (5 oz/155 g) coarsely chopped toasted pistachios

SERVES 8

In the spirit of brotherly competition, we went head-to-head trying to come up with the perfect halva recipe. Surprisingly, there seemed to be no definitive (or even good or workable) recipe for this Middle Eastern tahini-based dessert in any cookbook or online. Without a guide for success, we went in blind and relied on the flavor memories from our metro-Detroit youth and returned to our cooking roots. By completely making it up as we went along, we ended up with a perfect authentic halva. For all the frustration and crappy versions, the thrill of discovery was a rush. After we tasted it, yelled, and high-fived, we eagerly watched as people tasted it later that night.

Line the bottom and sides of a 9-inch (23-cm) square baking dish with parchment paper and coat the paper lightly with cooking spray. If the tahini has separated and has a layer of oil on top, pour off up to 2 tablespoons of the oil and discard.

In a saucepan, combine the sugar and 1 cup (8 fl oz/250 ml) water over medium-high heat and bring to a boil, stirring to dissolve the sugar. Reduce the heat to maintain a simmer and cook until the temperature registers 235°F (113°C) on a candy thermometer, about 10 minutes.

Meanwhile, in a small saucepan, warm the tahini and a pinch of salt over medium heat until it registers 110°F (43°C) on the candy thermometer, stirring to keep it well blended. Maintain the tahini at this temperature until the sugar syrup reaches at least 235°F. (If the temperature goes slightly higher, that's okay; the halva will just be a little more crumbly.)

In a heatproof bowl, combine the syrup, almond extract, pistachios, and warm tahini and gently stir with a silicone spatula until well blended. Continue stirring until the mixture cools to warm room temperature. As the mixture begins to cool, it will start to resemble a coarse dough and the oil will appear to separate; once it continues to cool, the mixture will come together again. At this point, using the silicone spatula, immediately transfer the mixture to the prepared pan, spreading it evenly and gently smoothing out the top. Let cool completely, then slice or break off chunks and serve. The halva will keep, tightly wrapped in the refrigerator, for about 1 week.

4 cups (32 fl oz/1 l) half-and-half

5 tea bags orange-and-spice flavored tea such as Constant Comment

½ cup (6 oz/185 ml) honey

Pinch of kosher salt

4 tsp powdered gelatin (a little less than 2 packets)

1 cup (3 oz/90 g) any kind of cookie crumbs except chocolate chip

---

In a saucepan, gently heat the half-and-half until very hot but not boiling. Stir constantly to prevent scorching.

Add the tea bags, honey, and salt and stir to dissolve the honey. Remove from the heat and let the tea steep until you like the balance of tea and milk flavors, usually 3–5 minutes. Remove the tea bags and squeeze the excess liquid into the pan. Set the pan aside.

Pour ¼ cup (2 fl oz/60 ml) cold water into a bowl. Sprinkle the gelatin over the water and let stand for 3–5 minutes to soften. Stir in 1 cup (8 fl oz/250 ml) of the steeped half-and-half. Pour the mixture back into the saucepan and stir to mix well.

Divide the panna cotta base evenly among eight ⅔-cup (160-ml) ramekins or small glasses, cover, and refrigerate until completely set, 2–3 hours.

To serve, sprinkle some of the cookie crumbs over each serving, then serve right away.

TEA
PANNA COTTA

SERVES 8

Like repainting the *Mona Lisa* with crayons, we could never do justice to our Grandma Claire's multilevel fruit-inside Jell-O desserts. But we do love a wonderful soft, jiggly dessert that's not too heavy and isn't the same ol' chocolatey-cake type of deal. This might be the easiest thing in the entire book to make. Crumbling crunchy cookies on top is the perfect contrast to the soft *panna cotta*. It ain't Jell-O, but we're sure our grandma would be proud.

AMARO ALMOND TRUFFLES

MAKES 20–25 TRUFFLES

In a different life, I once stood for hours in my underwear in a house in California in the middle of the summer and learned how to make state legal but federally illegal truffles. It was my Jesse Pinkman moment. The head baker of that operation offered his personal recipes to us, but we couldn't in good conscience republish them without the key ingredient. So while he does his thing his way, we've come up with a very easy truffle recipe with our own "secret" ingredient to take it up a notch. If you're new to the game, don't eat too many of these or you might get an extremely intense sugar high. — Eli

1 lb (500 g) dark chocolate chips (scant 3 cups)

2 Tbsp unsalted butter, at room temperature, cut into small pieces

½ cup (4 fl oz/125 ml) heavy cream

⅓ cup (3 fl oz/90 ml) amaro liqueur

1 tsp pure vanilla extract

1 cup (5½ oz/70 g) roasted almonds

Line a 5-inch (12-cm) square baking dish or heavy plastic container with parchment paper.

Put the chocolate in a heatproof bowl and nest the bowl in a saucepan over (not touching) simmering water. (Alternatively, put the chocolate in the top pan of a double boiler and place over simmering water in the lower pan.) Melt the chocolate, occasionally stirring gently with a silicone spatula to help it along. (Be careful not to let so much as a single drop of water get in your chocolate or it may seize.)

When the chocolate has fully melted, reduce the heat to low so the water is simmering very gently. Add the butter, a few pieces at a time and stirring with the spatula after each addition, until all of the butter is fully blended into the chocolate. The mixture should be smooth and velvety.

Switch to a whisk and slowly add the cream, whisking constantly until fully incorporated. Whisk in the amaro, about 1 tablespoon at a time, mixing well after each addition until evenly distributed. Whisk in the vanilla.

Remove the pan from the heat and whisk the entire mixture vigorously for 20 seconds. Pour into the prepared dish, let cool for 15 minutes, then refrigerate until set, about 3 hours.

In a food processor, pulse the almonds until uniformly finely ground. (Be careful not to overprocess, or they will turn into nut butter.) Transfer to a wide, shallow bowl and set aside at room temperature.

When the truffle base is set, remove it from the refrigerator. Line a sheet tray with parchment paper. Using the tip of a sharp knife, cut the truffle base into 1-inch (2.5-cm) squares. Lift out a square and roll it between your palms into a 1-inch (2.5-cm) ball. Gently roll the ball in the ground almonds until evenly coated and place on the prepared sheet tray. Repeat to make the remaining truffles.

Return the truffles to the fridge and chill for at least 15 minutes before serving. To store the truffles, transfer them to an airtight container and refrigerate for up to 4 days.

3 large eggs

2 cups (1 lb/500 g) sugar

3 Tbsp honey

1 cup (8 fl oz/250 ml) olive oil

½ cup (4 fl oz/125 ml) peanut or grapeseed oil

1½ cups (12 fl oz/375 ml) whole milk

2½ cups (12½/390 g) all-purpose flour

1 tsp kosher salt

½ tsp baking powder

½ tsp baking soda

½ cup (3 oz/90 g) almonds, coarsely chopped

Maple syrup for drizzling

Whipped cream or vanilla ice cream for serving

Preheat the oven to 375°F (190°C). Spray a 13-by-18-inch (33-by-46-cm) rimmed sheet tray with cooking spray.

In a food processor, combine the eggs, sugar, and honey and process until well blended, about 1 minute. With the machine running, in a slow, steady stream, add first the olive oil and then the peanut oil. The mixture should begin to thicken slightly but still be runny. Slowly add the milk and process for 1 minute.

In a large bowl, whisk together the flour, salt, baking powder, and baking soda, mixing well. Pour the wet ingredients into the dry ingredients and stir to mix well. The consistency should resemble a loose pancake batter.

Pour the batter into the prepared pan, making sure to scrape the edges of the bowl. Sprinkle the almonds evenly on top.

Bake for 10 minutes, then rotate the pan 180 degrees. Continue to bake until the top is golden brown and a toothpick inserted into the center comes out clean, about 10 minutes longer. If the batter sticks to the toothpick, bake for 5 more minutes.

Transfer to a wire rack and let cool completely in the pan. Drizzle with the maple syrup. Cut into pieces and serve, topped with whipped cream.

MAPLE SYRUP CAKE BARS

MAKES 12–16 BARS

One of the best parts about working in a restaurant is all the cool product around. And often when prepping for service, the extras make their way into a staff snack. After making the Mile End olive oil cake there was always a little extra batter. So as a snack for the staff, I stirred in some honey, poured some onto a sheet tray, and topped it with chopped nuts. Then once it was out of the oven, I drizzled maple syrup over the top. I wouldn't recommend treating the restaurant like your personal pantry as a way to get ahead, but do remember that a full staff is a happy staff. — Eli

DEEP-FRIED PB & J
SANDWICH WITH
WHITE CHOCOLATE GANACHE

Peanut oil for deep-frying

1 cup (6 oz/185 g) white chocolate chips

¼ cup (2 fl oz/60 ml) heavy cream

About ½ loaf good-quality raisin-walnut bread or similar heavy, sourdough-style nut or fruit bread

About ½ cup (5 oz/155 g) peanut butter

About ½ cup (5 oz/155 g) strawberry jam

About 2¼ cups (8 oz/250 g) banana chips

1 cup (5 oz/155 g) all-purpose flour

¼ cup (2 oz/60 g) sugar

1 tsp baking powder

1 tsp kosher salt

½ cup (4 fl oz/125 ml) milk

1 tsp pure vanilla extract

MAKES 4 SANDWICHES

PB&J sandwiches will now be guaranteed to silence your annoying child. This version not only calls for deep-frying the American staple but also takes it to a whole different realm of deliciousness with the addition of banana chips for crunch and white chocolate sauce for dipping. Although this would be insane trade bait in the lunchroom, it's best to eat these deep-fried wonders right out of the fryer.

Pour the oil to a depth of about 3 inches (7.5 cm) into a deep pot or deep fryer and heat to 325°F (165°C).

While the oil is heating, make the ganache. Put the chocolate in a heatproof bowl and nest the bowl in a saucepan over (not touching) simmering water. (Alternatively, put the chocolate in the top pan of a double boiler and place over simmering water in the lower pan.) Melt the chocolate, occasionally stirring gently with a silicone spatula to help it along. (Be careful not to let so much as a single drop of water get in your chocolate, or it may seize.) When the chocolate has fully melted, reduce the heat to low. Switch to a whisk and slowly add the cream, whisking constantly until fully incorporated. Remove the pan from the heat and pour the ganache into a heatproof bowl. Cover with aluminum foil to keep warm and set aside.

Cut the bread into 8 slices each about ¼ inch (6 mm) thick. Now, go ahead and make 4 peanut butter and jelly sandwiches. If you are a human, you should know how to do this. But for this fried version, be sure you don't overload them with too much PB or J! Before closing each sandwich, add a layer of the banana chips.

In a bowl, whisk together the flour, sugar, baking powder, and salt. Add the milk and vanilla and whisk until a smooth batter forms.

When the oil is hot, batter and fry the sandwiches one at a time. First, make sure all the sandwiches are tightly closed. Then, dip a sandwich into the batter and turn it gently to coat thoroughly. Lift it from the batter and let the excess batter drip back into the bowl. Use tongs to hold the sandwich tightly on one end, submerge it halfway into the hot oil and fry for 15 seconds, then release the sandwich into the oil. It should now float. Fry, turning once, until golden brown on both sides, about 2½ minutes per side. Using the tongs, transfer to paper towels to drain. Repeat to fry the remaining sandwiches.

Serve the sandwiches warm, with the warm ganache on the side for dipping.

FILL A SWIMMING POOL FULL OF BREAD AND DIVE INTO IT

In the restaurant world, pastry cooks have a different mentality from savory cooks. When you're cooking, you can season on the fly, adjust the heat as you go, and use a lot of tricks that can get you out of trouble if you make a mistake. With pastry, it's different. You have to measure everything to the gram and you can't exactly add a pinch of baking powder to a cake that's in the oven. Well, bread is like pastry, but add in the element of mystery, since no two breads ever bake up the same. Plus, yeast is actually a living element that acts differently based on the temperature, humidity, and a bunch of other factors. So, we admit that bread making can be tricky. But on the flip side, nothing really compares to the feeling of pulling a beautifully golden loaf out of the oven, waiting patiently until it cools, and then ripping into it, knowing that you made it from start to finish. It's a totally awesome skill to develop, and the best part is that most of the time is spent waiting, so you can bake bread even if you've got a lot of other stuff going on.

CHALLAH

MAKES TWO 2-LB (1-KG) LOAVES

1 package (2½ tsp) active dry yeast

1 tsp sugar or honey

2¼ cups (18 fl oz/560 ml) warm water (about 110°F/43°C)

½ cup (6 oz/185 ml) honey

⅔ cup (5 fl oz/160 ml) canola or vegetable oil

5 tsp kosher salt

Grated zest of 1 orange

Grated zest of 1 lemon

5 large eggs

1 cup (5 oz/155 g) whole-wheat flour

5–6 cups (25–30 oz/750–940 g) bread flour

3–4 Tbsp white sesame seeds or poppy seeds (optional)

In a small bowl, stir together the yeast, sugar, and ¼ cup (2 fl oz/60 ml) of the warm water and let stand until frothy, about 10 minutes.

Meanwhile, in a large bowl, whisk together the remaining 2 cups (16 fl oz/500 ml)

warm water, the honey, oil, salt, both zests, and 4 of the eggs until blended. Add the frothy yeast once ready. Add the whole-wheat flour, stirring it in with a spoon. Start adding the bread flour, 1 cup (5 oz/155 g) at a time, stirring it in with a spoon. When the dough becomes too stiff to work with the spoon, add the remainder of the flour up to 5 cups, mixing it in with your hands until incorporated.

To knead the dough, lightly flour a work surface and turn the dough out onto it. Put your hands on top of the dough, placing them on the part farthest from you. Grab about one-third of the mass and push it away from you slightly, then fold it back over onto itself. Push down with the heels of your hands firmly to stick the fold in place. Rotate the dough 90 degrees and repeat the pushing, folding, and sticking the fold in place. Continue this motion, keeping your work surface floured to prevent sticking, for 5–10 minutes. Use the remaining bread flour during the kneading process to prevent sticking. At the end of the kneading time, the dough should

be uniformly soft, smooth (not shaggy), elastic, and only slightly sticky. When you poke the dough with a finger, it should bounce back slightly.

Lightly oil a large bowl, put the dough in it, and cover the bowl with a kitchen towel. Let the dough rise in a warm, draft-free spot until about doubled in size, about 1 hour. (The timing will depend on the temperature of the water you used and the ambient temperature in the room.)

Preheat the oven to 375°F (190°C). Line a large baking sheet with parchment paper.

Lightly flour the work surface and turn the dough out onto it. Divide the dough into 6 equal pieces. Using the same kneading technique, knead each piece into a smooth ball, keeping the pieces you are not working with covered with a kitchen towel. Now, roll each ball into a rope about 10 inches (25 cm) long: First, clean the work surface so that it has little to no flour on it. Then, using your palms in a back-and-forth motion, work the first ball a little to start to shape the rope, then go to the next ball and work it a little. Proceed in this manner, working on each piece of dough in rotation (as opposed to rolling a single piece to full length before moving on to the next one), until all of the ropes are formed. Working this way gives the gluten time to relax, which makes the ropes easier to form.

To shape the challah, on the work surface, line up 3 ropes of dough parallel to one another and positioned vertically to you. Pinch together the ends farthest from you, then braid the ropes, stretching them slightly as you work to maintain smoothness. Pinch the bottom ends together and carefully lift the braid onto half of the prepared pan. Tuck the top and bottom ends under. Repeat with the remaining 3 ropes to make the second loaf.

In a small bowl, whisk together the remaining 1 egg with 1 tablespoon water to make an egg wash. Brush each loaf with the egg wash, then sprinkle generously with the seeds, if using.

Bake the loaves, rotating the pan 180 degrees halfway through the baking, until golden brown, about 45 minutes. Transfer the loaves to a wire rack and let cool completely before slicing. The loaves can be frozen for up to 2 weeks.

FOCACCIA

MAKES ONE 13-BY-18-INCH (33-BY-46-CM) SHEET

Sponge
⅛ tsp active dry yeast
½ cup (4 fl oz/125 ml) cool water
½ cup (2½ oz/75 g) bread flour

Dough
2 tsp active dry yeast
1¼ cups (10 fl oz/310 ml) cool water
¼ cup (2 fl oz/60 ml) extra-virgin olive oil, plus 2 Tbsp

¼ cup (1½ oz/45 g) whole-wheat flour
2 Tbsp chopped fresh rosemary
1 Tbsp kosher salt
3⅓–3⅔ cups (17–19 oz/530–590 g) bread flour, or more if needed

To make the sponge, in a bowl, stir together the yeast, water, and flour, loosely cover with plastic wrap, and let stand until bubbles form on the surface, 3–6 hours at room temperature or overnight in the refrigerator.

To make the dough, in a large bowl, stir together the yeast and water, then stir in the ¼ cup (2 fl oz/60 ml) olive oil. Whisk in the whole-wheat flour, rosemary, and salt, then beat in the sponge and as much of the bread flour as needed to make a dough that is sticky but holds together and forms a ball. Cover the bowl with a kitchen towel and let the dough rise in a warm, draft-free spot until doubled in size, 1–2 hours.

Preheat the oven to 400°F (200°C). Brush a 13-by-18-inch (33-by-46-cm) sheet tray with the 2 tablespoons olive oil.

When the dough is ready, turn it out onto the prepared pan. Handling the dough as little as possible to maintain the bubbles, stretch it to the edges of the pan, working to create an even thickness without spots that are either too thin or thick.

Bake until the top is golden brown, about 35 minutes. Let cool slightly in the pan on a wire rack, then cut into squares and serve.

SESAME SEMOLINA BREAD
(adapted from Jim Leahy's no knead dough)

MAKES ONE 1½-LB (750-G) LOAF
1½ cups (8 oz/250 g) semolina flour
1½ cups (5 oz/155 g) bread flour plus more for dusting
½ tsp active dry yeast

2 tsp salt
1½ cups (12 fl oz/375 ml) cool water
¼ cup (1 oz/30 g) white sesame seeds

In a large bowl, whisk together the semolina and bread flours, the yeast, and the salt. Add the cool water and stir to combine, forming a loose, shaggy dough ball. Let stand at room temperature for 1–2 hours, depending on ambient temperature, then cover with plastic wrap and refrigerate overnight.

In the morning, the dough will have risen and bubbles will be visible on the surface. Remove from the refrigerator and let come to room temperature in a warm place for 1 hour

Dust a work surface with the bread flour. Turn out the dough onto the floured surface and fold it over onto itself 3 or 4 times, until it forms a ball. Sprinkle a kitchen towel with a generous layer of bread flour. Put the ball of dough, seam side down, on the towel. Dust with more flour, then cover with another kitchen towel or fold the bottom towel gently over the top. Let the dough rise in a warm spot until doubled in size, 1–2 hours.

Place a 6-qt (6-l) Dutch oven or other heavy-bottomed ovenproof pot with a lid in the oven and preheat to 450°F (230°C).

When the dough is ready, remove the pot from the oven. Carefully turn the dough over, seam side up, into the preheated pot. Mist the top of the dough with water and sprinkle the sesame seeds evenly over the top. Shake the pot once or twice to distribute the dough if very uneven, but it will straighten out as it bakes. Cover the pot with the lid.

Bake for 30 minutes, then remove the lid and continue to bake until the loaf is nicely browned, 15 to 30 minutes longer. Turn the bread out onto a wire rack and let cool for at least 1 hour before slicing.

MORE RANDOM STUFF

That you can cook to forever change your life.

PICKLED RINDS

MAKES 1 PINT (16 FL OZ/500 ML)

Rind from ¼ large watermelon, red flesh trimmed off with ⅛ inch of white flesh intact

½ cup (4 fl oz/125 ml) distilled white vinegar

2 Tbsp rice vinegar

1 Tbsp sugar

1 Tbsp kosher salt

In a plastic container with a tight-fitting lid, combine the watermelon rind, both vinegars, the sugar, the salt, and ½ cup (4 fl oz/125 ml) water. Cover tightly, shake well to dissolve the sugar and salt, and refrigerate for at least 4 hours or preferably overnight. To use the rinds, remove them from the brine and, using a mandoline or a sharp knife, slice lengthwise to desired thickness. (The rinds will keep for up to 2 weeks.)

MISO AIOLI

MAKES ABOUT 2 CUPS (16 FL OZ/500 ML)

2 Tbsp white miso

1 tsp peeled and minced fresh ginger

1 Tbsp fresh lime juice, or to taste

2 large egg yolks

2 cups (16 fl oz/500 ml) vegetable oil

1 Tbsp thinly sliced fresh chives

Kosher salt

To prevent the aioli from breaking, that is, separating into liquid and partially solid parts, make sure all of the ingredients are cold and do not add the oil too quickly. In a food processor or blender, combine the miso, ginger, lime juice, and egg yolks and process until smooth. With the machine running, begin adding the vegetable oil drop by drop. Then, as the mixture emulsifies and thickens, add the remaining oil in a slow, steady drizzle until all of the oil is incorporated and the mixture is the consistency of mayonnaise. If the mixture is too thick, add a few drops of ice water to thin it out slightly. Fold in the chives and season with salt. Use immediately, or transfer to an airtight container and refrigerate for up to 1 week.

ROASTED GARLIC DRESSING

MAKES ABOUT ¾ CUP (6 FL OZ/180 ML)

1 head garlic, cloves separated and unpeeled

Extra-virgin olive oil to cover, plus ½ cup (4 fl oz/125 ml)

Juice of 2 lemons

1 tsp ground cumin

Kosher salt and freshly ground pepper

In a small saucepan, combine the garlic cloves with oil to cover and bring to a gentle simmer over medium heat. Reduce the heat to low and cook gently until a paring knife meets no resistance when thrust through a clove, about 30 minutes. Remove the pan from the heat.

Using a slotted spoon, transfer the cloves to a bowl and let them cool until they can be handled. (Discard the poaching oil or save for another use.) Peel the cooled cloves and place in a food processor or blender. Add the ½ cup (4 fl oz/125 ml) olive oil, the lemon juice, cumin, 1 teaspoon salt, and ¼ teaspoon pepper and process until smooth. Taste and adjust the seasoning. Use immediately, or transfer to an airtight container and refrigerate for up to 3 days.

TERIYAKI SAUCE

MAKES ABOUT 1¾ CUPS (14 FL OZ/430 ML)

2 Tbsp olive oil

1 head garlic, cloves separated and thinly sliced

1 shallot, thinly sliced

2-inch (5-cm) piece fresh ginger, peeled and thinly sliced

1 bunch green onions, white and tender green parts only, trimmed and roughly chopped

1 whole organic orange, unpeeled, roughly chopped

¾ cup (6 fl oz/180 ml) mirin

½ cup (4 fl oz/125 ml) chicken stock

1 cup (8 fl oz/250 ml) soy sauce

1 Tbsp sambal oelek chili sauce

In a saucepan, warm the olive oil over medium-low heat. Add the garlic, shallot, ginger, and green onions and stir to coat with the oil. Cook, stirring occasionally, until dark and caramelized and even a bit burned in parts, 10–15 minutes. Add the orange, mirin, stock, soy sauce, and chili sauce and stir to mix. Simmer until thickened slightly, about 20 minutes.

Remove from the heat, strain through a fine-mesh sieve into a heatproof bowl, and let cool. Use immediately, or store in an airtight container in the refrigerator for up to 1 month.

SPICY TOMATO JAM

MAKES ABOUT 1 PINT (16 FL OZ/500 ML)

1 large yellow onion, sliced

2 Tbsp extra-virgin olive oil

3 lb (1.5 kg) plum tomatoes

1 clove garlic, chopped

¼ cup (2 fl oz/60 ml) sherry vinegar

1 cup (8 oz/250 g) sugar

2 tsp kosher salt

½ tsp cayenne pepper

Preheat the oven to 450°F (230°C). In a large bowl, toss the onion slices with 1 tablespoon of the olive oil. Spread in a single layer on one end of a large sheet tray. Toss the tomatoes with the remaining 1 tablespoon olive oil and arrange in a single layer on the rest of the sheet tray.

Transfer the pan to the oven and roast the tomatoes until the skins start to peel, about 10 minutes. Remove from the oven and, using tongs, transfer the tomatoes to a large plate or tray. Use the tongs to toss and turn the onion slices a bit and spread them in a single layer again. Return the pan to the oven and continue roasting until the onion slices are tender and nicely golden brown, about 20 minutes longer.

When the tomatoes are cool enough to handle, peel off and discard the skins. Core and halve the tomatoes, then discard the inner membranes and seeds. Roughly chop the onion.

In a saucepan, combine the tomatoes, onion, garlic, vinegar, sugar, salt, and cayenne and bring to a simmer over medium heat, stirring often. Cook until the tomatoes have broken down and softened, about 30 minutes. Remove from the heat. Using an immersion blender, blend all of the ingredients until finely and uniformly chopped. Return the pan to low heat, bring to a very gentle simmer, and cook until thickened, 1–1½ hours longer.

Remove from the heat and taste and adjust the seasoning. Let cool, then transfer the jam to an airtight container and refrigerate for up to 1 month.

CURRY POWDER

MAKES ABOUT ⅔ CUP (2¼ OZ/65 G)

2 Tbsp *each* whole cumin seeds and whole coriander seeds

1 Tbsp whole mustard seeds

1 tsp *each* whole cardamom seeds and whole black peppercorns

¼ cup (¼ oz/7 g) ground turmeric

2 tsp cayenne pepper

1 tsp ground ginger

In a small, dry frying pan, combine the cumin, coriander, mustard, cardamom, and peppercorns over medium heat and toast, stirring constantly, until the seeds pop, smoke slightly, and are very fragrant, 3–5 minutes.

Pour the toasted seeds onto a sheet tray and spread them out to cool. When the seeds have cooled completely, working in batches, grind them in a spice grinder or clean coffee grinder to a fine powder. As you work, transfer the batches to a bowl.

Add the turmeric, cayenne, and ginger to the ground spices and stir to mix thoroughly. Store the curry powder in an airtight container in a cool, dark place until ready to use. The potency will begin to fade after a week or so, but the powder will still be tasty for up to 1 month.

MEXICAN CHORIZO

MAKES ABOUT 1 LB (500 G)

1 lb (500 g) ground pork

6 cloves garlic, minced

2 tsp red wine vinegar

2 tsp packed light brown sugar

1 Tbsp kosher salt

1 Tbsp dried oregano

2 tsp *each* smoked paprika, ancho chile powder, chipotle chile powder, and ground cumin

1 tsp cayenne pepper

½ tsp ground coriander

In a large bowl, combine the pork, garlic, vinegar, and brown sugar. Stir briefly to distribute the garlic evenly.

In a small bowl, whisk together the salt, oregano, paprika, chile powders, cumin, cayenne, and coriander until thoroughly blended. Add to the pork mixture and stir to mix.

Heat a frying pan over medium-high heat. Pinch off a small piece of the meat mixture and fry in the hot pan until browned and cooked through. Taste and adjust the seasoning of the mixture, if necessary. Repeat to cook the remaining meat mixture.

Use right away or store, wrapped loosely, in the refrigerator for up to 2 days.

INDEX

FROM MAX AND ELI

This cookbook is dedicated to our grandfather Ed Avadenka, the toughest and most loving family man we'll ever know. We'll keep it short and sweet just the way you like it: We miss you and hope you are proud.

THANK YOU TO

OUR EVER-SUPPORTIVE PARENTS for lending an ear to our endless barrage of complaining and supporting us through our uncertainty and concerns; you'll always be the unsung partners of all our endeavors.

NANA AND PAPA for showing us what being the best at something truly looks like.

AMY MARR the best publisher ever! Here's to a brief reprieve from chasing us down via email for a new header, anecdote, recipe fix, and a million other things you did to pull this baby together.

EMMA BOYS AND THE CREATIVE TEAM you guys really got our vision! Thanks for delivering a cover and interiors that make us incredibly proud.

MEGAN AMRAM for being hilarious. PAY YOUR TAXES ALREADY JESUS.

AUNT BETH for testing a bunch of recipes and providing excellent, enlightening feedback!

OUR ENTIRE FAMILY for the love and support that keeps us going; we hope we did you proud again.

GONZALO AND THE MARKETING TEAM for pushing this book and doing all the hard, not-that-fun work that you do every day.

SIMON ANDREWS "much more than a stylist" should be your slogan. We absolutely could not have done this book without you.

ERIN KUNKEL you make everything look so much better than it is. Thanks for keeping it light, fun, and fresh and delivering a stellar body of work for BCE.

PAIGE HICKS for killing it again with the setups. Your stuff is the best!

SOREN we'll cook dinner if you get us tickets to Kascade. Fair trade? Thanks for your editing expertise.

SHAY, EDDIE, REBECCA, RIE, AND CHRIS for all your hard work on this project!

MEGHAN "GROUNDHOG" MACKENZIE thanks for always looking out for us. Here's to many more, in many more mediums.

DR. NOAH "BLAZE" BERMANOFF an awesome boss, a great friend. Thanks for being cool as fuck.

JJ you are simply the best. (but 3 cats is still too many though).

KATE "TACOS FIESTA" MCCABE ACAPULCO!!!!!!

MAX "CHAMPAGNE BUBBLE BATH" ARONSON for keeping me grounded and honest.

COLIN for your brainstorming genius.

MURPHY THE CHILEAN CHILI CONEY DOG we wish you could talk SO BAD. Please just start talking.

ALL OUR DINNER PARTY PEEPS Ali, Ashley, Davesh, Dirty Diana, Kate, Keith, Neanna, Ora, Youngmi, Dave Laven, D, Masha, Erin, and Ebenezer—thanks for looking mighty fine and barely eating for a long long time.

ALL OUR RECIPE TESTERS too many to name here, but you were instrumental to making this book work.

JEAN ARMSTRONG AND EVERYONE AT WILLIAMS-SONOMA for the opportunity. Again. We feel honored to sit on your shelves.

CHRISTOPHER BASTIAN, DOUG GELLER, AND EVERYONE AT GANT we would have never, under any circumstances, looked this good without you.

Olive Press

Recipes and text © Copyright 2013
Eli Sussman and Max Sussman

Images and illustrations © Copyright 2013
Weldon Owen, Inc.

Olive Press is an imprint of
Weldon Owen, Inc. and Williams-Sonoma, Inc.

Weldon Owen, Inc. is a division of Bonnier Corporation

415 Jackson Street, Suite 200, San Francisco, CA 94111

Library of Congress Control Number: 2013951241

ISBN 13: 978-1-61628-635-4
ISBN 10: 1-61628-635-0

www.weldonowen.com

www.williams-sonoma.com

Printed and bound in the USA

First printed in 2013
10 9 8 7 6 5 4 3 2 1